Terry Haller teaches strategy at Keller Graduate School of Management in Chicago. He is president of the Chicago Research Company, chairman of the Financial Communications Center, an editor of the *Journal of Business Strategy*, and a member of the Advisory Committee of Innovators and Entrepreneurs Institute.

THE SUCCESSFUL STRATEGIST
A 90-Minute Guide to Corporate Power

Terry Haller

A SPECTRUM BOOK

Prentice-Hall, Inc., Englewood Cliffs, N.J. 07632

Library of Congress Cataloging in Publication Data

HALLER, TERRY.
   The successful strategist.
   ("A Spectrum Book.")
   Includes index.
   1. Corporate planning.   2. Control (Psychology)
I. Title.
HD30.28.H342   1984   658.4'012   84-11623
ISBN 0-13-872748-1
ISBN 0-13-872730-9 (pbk.)

This book is available at a special discount when ordered
in bulk quantities. Contact Prentice-Hall, Inc., General
Publishing Division, Special Sales, Englewood Cliffs, N.J. 07632.

© 1984 by Prentice-Hall, Inc., Englewood Cliffs, New Jersey 07632

Manufacturing buyer: Patrick Mahoney
Cover design © 1984 by Jeannette Jacobs

A SPECTRUM BOOK

ISBN 0-13-872748-1

ISBN 0-13-872730-9 {PBK.}

10 9 8 7 6 5 4 3 2 1

Printed in the United States of America

PRENTICE-HALL INTERNATIONAL, INC., *London*
PRENTICE-HALL OF AUSTRALIA PTY. LIMITED, *Sydney*
PRENTICE-HALL CANADA, INC., *Toronto*
PRENTICE-HALL OF INDIA PRIVATE LIMITED, *New Delhi*
PRENTICE-HALL OF JAPAN, INC., *Tokyo*
PRENTICE-HALL OF SOUTHEAST ASIA PTE. LTD., *Singapore*
WHITEHALL BOOKS LIMITED, *Wellington, New Zealand*
EDITORA PRENTICE-HALL DO BRASIL LTDA., *Rio de Janeiro*

For Anna, my equal opportunity
wife at time of writing

Contents

Why I Wrote This Book   xiii

Why You Must Read This Book (Before It's Too Late)   xv

Part I
**ALL YOU NEED TO KNOW ABOUT BUSINESS
STRATEGY   1**

chapter one
Why We Make Lousy Strategists   3

chapter two
The Boring Bits   6

chapter three
The Single Most Important Thing About Strategy   8

chapter four
Meet the Advertising Boys   11

chapter five
No Empty Talk   14

chapter six
But What Is It?   18

chapter seven
Why Quality Is Nice   22

chapter eight
Being Different for a Reason   26

chapter nine
What Price Do I Set?   30

chapter ten
Pricing New Products   35

chapter eleven
Do I Have a Value for You   38

chapter twelve
Growth Markets: The Good and the Bad   41

chapter thirteen
DUH Take   48

chapter fourteen
The New Product 52

chapter fifteen
R & D 57

chapter sixteen
Segmenting Onward 62

chapter seventeen
Manufacturing Strategy 65

chapter eighteen
Financial Strategy 74

chapter nineteen
Mergers and Acquisitions 79

chapter twenty
Incentives 82

chapter twenty-one
The Corporate Matrix 84

chapter twenty-two
Stock Prices 89

chapter twenty-three
Compulsory Chapter on Japanese Management Modes 92

Part II
THE POWER 95

chapter twenty-four
Power: How Not to Get It 97

chapter twenty-five
What Should the Strategist Know About Power? 102

chapter twenty-six
Arranging to Get Power 105

chapter twenty-seven
Implementing Your Power Plan with Examples 108

chapter twenty-eight
Is Strategy a Team Task? 110

chapter twenty-nine
Strategic Management 114

chapter thirty
Things Will Be Great for the Strategist 117

Part III
POWER PLAYS FOR WOMEN 119

chapter thirty-one
Do Women Make Good Strategists? 121

chapter thirty-two
Can the Network Help?   124

chapter thirty-three
Shaping the Strategic Personna   128

Index   135

Why I Wrote This Book

I wrote this book because I got angry at all the business books flooding the market. Books that give guys like me a bad name. Most of these books are just sugar pills. You're tricked into buying them, lured by promises of becoming a raving success with one easy trick. But they cheat you with naive perspectives. You end up feeling bilked. You know business success isn't that easy.

Maybe, like me, you've come to realize the ultimate business truth: The only thing that really counts is your strategy—not tactics that in the end are not all that critical. Business is strategy. And strategy is power. Whether you're smart or stupid, if you haven't got a handle on strategy, you'll never have any power.

Unfortunately, most individuals don't know much about strategy. Accordingly, they remain powerless and underpaid tacticians for their entire careers.

Fortunately, they now can read this book. And in 90 minutes be on the road to corporate power.

Why You Must Read This Book (Before It's Too Late)

You must read this book because what you want more than anything else is power.

Come on, don't pretend to be innocent. It's not the money you're working for. That's not enough for you. Admit it. And it's not because you love your job. Don't make me laugh.

It's power that drives you. "Power is the ultimate aphrodisiac," said Henry Kissinger. Power is what satisfies your ego. Power is what people respect—maybe the only thing.

If you work for a corporation, whether it's big or small, power gives you control: control over the company, over its employees, and over your own fate.

If you don't have corporate power, you're a sitting duck. You can't have security. Without power you aren't calling the shots. Someone else is. Power gives you control over your own career, over your own fate.

This book tells you how to get corporate power. (Once having gotten that, community power will follow as naturally as night follows day.)

Corporate power does not go to those with good looks, charm, and a manipulative personality—except by default. All those books that tell you how to acquire power by the sheer force of your personality work only in a corporate vacuum. There is a better way to get power. And if you feel you lack the superficial attributes of charm and personality, you are in luck having found this book.

The fast lane to power lies in making yourself the corporation's most resourceful source of success. Business success is what counts in the end. That's why the shareholders invested in the company, and that's what they expect. Shareholders don't invest in a company because of its products, its location, its industry, or anything else. They invest in its strategy. It's a company's strategy that will, in the end, make or break it. It is the strategy that is the company's destiny.

Corporate power goes to those who have learned how to formulate business strategies that produce success. It does not go to failures or to people who cannot demonstrate that they will satisfy the shareholders. Shareholders want results, not charm, and results flow from clever strategies. They don't come from anywhere else.

This book is written in three parts. The first part tells you what you need to know about business strategy. In plain, nonjargon terms, it reveals the principal laws of business strategy—giving you the weapons you need to make yourself indispensable. If you know strategy, you become invulnerable to your rivals' gambits against you in the quest for corporate power. The second part tells you how to use this strategy lore to plot your course to the pinnacle of power. The third part is for women and offers concrete proposals to facilitate their career planning and quest for corporate recognition and power.

Power. After all is said and done, it's what we are all after. Without power, life is not really worth living. Without the tools of strategy, power is out of reach. With the knowledge of the secrets of strategy, power can be yours faster than you may think.

I

ALL YOU NEED TO KNOW ABOUT BUSINESS STRATEGY

Business strategy governs the way all the resources—physical, financial, and human—of an enterprise are to be used. Those who know how to forge business strategies wield exceptional power, for they hold the secret to the success of the enterprise. The power that comes with the knowledge of business strategy outranks any other kind of power—except out-and-out ownership of the corporation.

Before exercising this power, you must first learn all about the laws of business strategy. This, then, is your homework. You must finish it before going on to Part II, which deals with the way you will capitalize on your new-found knowledge to seize the reins of power.

1

chapter one
Why We Make
Lousy Strategists

"Let me answer him," interjected Link, looking straight at Digby Bunkman and puffing himself up like a princely frog. "Bunkie, if the American Foundryland is to be revived, we're going to have to do it ourselves—our study group, our graduating class, our alma mater. We'll have to apply our sublime intellects to the task. Our nation is counting on us." Link Dover waxed eloquent when the fate of the nation was at stake.

—T. Haller, *Link Dover at Harvard Business School* [1]

Most of us make lousy business strategists, and I think I know why. The reason came to light while I was listening to a talk show. The host was discussing World War II trivia. He asked his listeners if they could name the only American who received both the Medal of Honor and the Pulitzer Prize. A lot of people called in with wrong answers such as Ernie Pyle. Finally, a woman got it right.

"Charles Lindbergh," she said.

[1]Terry Haller, "Link Dover at Harvard Business School," (Unpublished manuscript, 1984). Used with permission throughout.

3

"Correct," announced the host. "Say, do you happen to recall what he got the Pulitzer for?"

"Aviation," she answered.

"No, I'm afraid not," said the host. "The Pulitzer is awarded for writing."

"Oh," she replied, "I never knew Lindbergh wrote anything."

In a flash I had the answer to the riddle: "Why do we make such crummy strategists?" It's because we are suckers for instant analysis.

The caller was half-cocked. She didn't even comprehend the question. It may be amusing that she still had the right answer. But in the business world when we reach a strategic crossroads, we can be right half the time by just flipping a coin. Unfortunately, being right only half the time isn't good enough—not when your goal is corporate power.

Our country is in bad shape. The reason for its trouble is that we have deluded ourselves into thinking strategy is simpler than it really is. The way we tackle strategy reminds me of those news commentators who dish out instant analysis immediately following the presidential debates. I think many of us actually believe that only wimps have to analyze and think for a bit before arriving at a major strategic decision.

We're used to pontificating on game strategy after watching an NFL game. Everybody who saw the game can be an expert. If football is just business in a different form, then the art of business strategy is an open game for anyone.

Well, if you believe that about business strategy, then this book is going to be an eye-opener. There's a lot more to business strategy than there is to gridiron strategy. It's not something you can get into successfully without some degree of preparation. It just doesn't compare to a lock-erroom post-mortem.

But relax. This book will make it all very simple. It'll show you the important components of strategy and how they work together. And it should take you only about 90 minutes to read it all the way through. In other words, if you read it during the commercial breaks of two NFL games, you should be able to finish it.

chapter two
The Boring Bits

"Okay," said Bunkie, "Let's get on with it."
T. Haller, *Link Dover at Harvard Business School*

No self-respecting, instructional book can be complete without some boring definitions. It's dirty work, but someone's got to do it. So let's get it over with.

Business strategy is when you put all your resources together in a way that lets you prosper in your particular business environment. Your physical resources include office, plants, equipment, and stuff like this. But you also have other resources. For example, the money you kicked in and the dough you borrowed from your brother-in-law. Also the brains of all the wonderful folks who work for you. They're your human resources. The environment is the industry your business happens to be in. And along with that goes its economic climate.

A shorter definition of business strategy is "doing the right things in the right business." However, that won't mean much to you until you read this book.

While we're at it, let's get the SBU out of the way. *SBU* stands for "strategic business unit." All it really means is that before you start planning a business strategy, you have to deal with the smallest piece of the business possible.

Here's an example. Let's pretend you make a line of shampoos. You'd probably have a regular shampoo, a dandruff shampoo, and maybe some with conditioners in them. Your SBU wouldn't be the whole ball of wax. There'd be a separate SBU for dandruff shampoos and so forth. You have strategic flexibility in each SBU. You can advertise more and promote more on the dandruff product without having to do the same thing on the regular product. Each SBU is strategically independent. So naturally you don't want to put them all into the same pot.

I've seen fights break out when people try to decide on their SBUs. For some reason deciding seems to attract the nit-pickers. You really shouldn't have to think too long about it. If you manage to stay awake from nine to five, it should be obvious to you which is an SBU and which isn't.

Now for the last boring bit. Strategy has several different components. You've got to analyze these pieces separately before you can put them back together in the form of a successful strategy. Each of these major components is covered in a separate chapter.

Whew. I'm glad we got all that over with. From here on the book gets more interesting.

chapter three
The Single Most Important Thing About Strategy

It is a silly game where nobody wins.

Thomas Fuller, *Gnomologia*, No. 2880.

Quick, what do IBM, the Pope, and Colombian cocaine dealers have in common? Give up? It's that all have dominant market shares. Market share is spelled C-L-O-U-T.

Market share is strategy's most important component. Have you ever figured out what your share is? Even with flimsy raw data it's not hard to calculate. It's just the percentage your business has of the total market. For strategy purposes, a rough estimate will do nicely.

First, you're going to have to define your market. To Budweiser and Miller, the market is the whole country. But if your locality is still blessed with a homegrown brewhouse, its market is probably viewed just as the immediate vicinity. If your kid makes pocket money cutting lawns, his market is the neighborhood. Get it? The market is where you actually compete.

Now for something completely different—the first of my MagiCubes. You are ordered to commit these charts to memory! The MagiCubes show the combined impact of two strategy components on profits. Profit here means return-on-investment.

For the sake of simplicity, we'll use a movie-rating system: One star means an ROI of 10% or under, two stars mean 11 to 15%, three stars mean 16 to 20%, and anything with more than a 20% ROI is a monster, four-star box-office success. Once in a long while I'll use five stars; that's when the ROI approaches or exceeds 30%—a very rare occurrence indeed.

Our first chart no doubt answers the question that came to your mind as soon as we started the market share business: "Does market share really count if my business is small?"

MAGICUBE 1

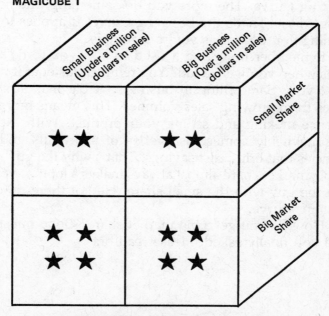

BUSINESS SIZE AND MARKET SHARE

The first rule of strategy is covered in the following Strateg-O-Gram:

YOU CANNOT ESCAPE THE CLOUT OF MARKET SHARE.

Market share is directly tied to profit, regardless of your size. There are reasons for this of course. The bigger your share, the bigger your sales volume. This gives an economy of scale that your lower-share competitors don't have. So you make more money per sales unit than they do.

You also have greater bargaining power in the market. It makes your distributors feature your product more prominently. They know there's a strong demand for it. They know which side their bread is buttered on.

But the biggest reason of all is something they call the Learning Curve. The more you do something, the better you get at it. That's the Learning Curve. It applies to everything you do unless you're a zombie.

Remember how long it used to take you to tie your shoes when you were a kid? You're much faster at it now, aren't you? Same thing in business. A big market share comes from growing sales volumes. This means more experience making and selling your product. With experience inevitably comes discoveries of short-cuts and efficiencies that bring cost savings. That's why the guy with the big market share almost always makes a lot more profit than the guy with the small share. He got there riding a Learning Curve.

How do you get a big market share? Good question. Glad you finally asked. Please read on.

chapter four
Meet the Advertising Boys

Go, hang yourselves all! you are idle shallow things: I am
not of your element.

Shakespeare, *Twelfth Night*, III-iv

Getting a big market share is easy to talk about. But hard
to do, otherwise everybody would have one. Still, it's not
impossible. There are strategic share-building approaches
that give very good odds. Unfortunately, too many businesses simply follow tactical courses in quest of big market
shares.

There are more tactics than widows at a sultan's fu-
neral. Tactics are more fun than strategies. That's the
trouble with strategy—it hardly makes engaging luncheon
conversation. I found this out at the University Club one
afternoon. I had booked lunch there with some ad agency
biggies. I'm sure you know the type.

The nice thing about the University Club is its Gothic
dining room. It's like an old cathedral. Everything you say
in there sounds like you're reading it off a scroll. Thus, my
luncheon companions couldn't resist the temptation to

11

pontificate—especially when I asked them if anything new was happening on the market-share frontier.

"Look," said the oldest, "there is magic hidden in every product. Our job is finding it and telling consumers about it."

"Right," chimed in his fast-talking cohort, "except this magic doesn't have to be anything you can smell, taste, or touch. What I mean is this: A clever commercial can get consumers to look at the product in a different, more favorable light."

"Find out what the consumer wants. Do your research," said the elder agency statesman.

"Then, through your advertising, make them believe you satisfy that need," added the younger.

"Don't you guys ever want to know about the product itself?" I asked.

"Oh sure. I'll even take it home and use it. But essentially all products are pretty dull. It's our job to make them sexy," I was told.

"It's just old-fashioned salesmanship—creating a need and supplying the answer to that need. Salesmanship is the force that propels our entire economy," said the senior wordsmith.

"Or today we call it marketing to include the more sophisticated parts of salesmanship. The research. The commercials. The media buys. Marketing is the most critical function of the business world," added the junior adman.

"Then I guess you wouldn't agree with what Francis Cuppola said?" I inquired.

"The guy who directed 'The Godfather'? What did he say?"

"He said, 'Marketing—a word that singlehandedly destroyed Detroit.' "[1]

[1]"All Things Considered," National Public Radio, Feb. 9, 1982.

"What did he mean—that he didn't like marketing? I don't get it," said the elder.

"I think it's plain. All the research, the fancy commercials, and the humungous media budgets couldn't help Detroit stave off the Japanese auto," I answered softly.

Silence fell upon the Gothic dining room. I signed for lunch.

After I left the University Club, I headed north on Michigan Avenue, then paused a while on the bridge, looking for the goldfish in the deep green murk of the Chicago River. You could still see them—giant goldfish swimming around the piles. Some things never change—the Chicago River goldfish, despite the pollution; ad men, despite the horrid realities of the economy.

As far as I was concerned, the answer, as always, was strategy. The tactical side had nothing new to offer. Just the same old voodoo and black magic. Not the kind of stuff that's going to help us beat the Russians.

There are ways of getting a bigger market share. But you don't do it by hoodwinking the customer. That never works for long. You can't build your business empire on one-shot strategies. You want to develop a customer franchise. You want folks coming back for more. The ad agency boys seldom throught much beyond consumer trial. They were hung up on getting consumers to try the product. And they found that it was fairly easy. They just did it with big promises. But unless you deliver the goods, you never get what you really need from the consumer—repeat business. Promises don't make them buy your product a second time.

chapter five
No Empty Talk

"Let me give it a wack," exclaimed Bunkie, underlining parts of the mimeographed Smokestack Flange Corp. case problem with a yellow crayon. "What we have here is just another sick flange company that needs a hot Madison Avenue ad shop. To give it an image and to give it a halo effect to add sex appeal to some pretty lousy products."
"Won't work, old bean," Link said patiently. "Been tried before. Many times. That's what got them in trouble in the first place."

T. Haller, *Link Dover at Harvard Business School*

You don't want to hear about my wife's washing machine. I don't either. But I still hear about it. Seems it doesn't get the dirt out. Not even half as well as her 15-year old Frigidaire they took as a trade-in. To my ad agency friends I guess this matter is immaterial. Their part in this matter was successful. Their ads made my wife buy that machine. But they didn't make her happy. And she's never going to buy anything made by that company again.

This story brings up a key strategy used to boost market shares. It's called "quality." While this may sound more like a Sunday sermon than a serious business message, I do mean it. A quality strategy gives you a bigger market share, and bigger profits. This is a fact.

If you took all the businesses in the country and split them into low and high share groups, you'd see something pretty impressive about quality. First, half the low share businesses would have products with poor quality. Another quarter would have average quality. And yet another quarter would have high quality. Second, the high share group would be a mirror image of this. Fully half its businesses would have high quality products. Get the picture?

I gave a talk in New York City about this. When I got to this part someone in the audience said, "Hell, anyone can do that. It's just buying share. Any fool can unload diamonds at zircon prices."

New Yorkers always think they can stump us hayseeds from the Second City. This time I disappointed them. My next slide was ready. What it showed is what I've put on MagiCube 2. Take a quick look.

Doesn't it demolish the abrasive New Yorker? High share folks who also have high quality just happen to get the fattest ROIs. Obviously, you don't make big profits by giving your goods away. High share, high quality, and fat profits all go hand-in-hand. That's a business law.

It's also more bad news for Marxists. Because it says in our free enterprise system the greatest rewards go to firms producing the best products. It's even good medicine for a small-share business. This business does a lot better in the profit department with high quality than with low quality.

Maybe we'll never get an American automobile we'll be perfectly happy with. Perhaps that's impossible. But these days the quality strategy is a big deal in Detroit. There's even been some progress.

For example, at Ford's assembly plant in Louisville,

MAGICUBE 2

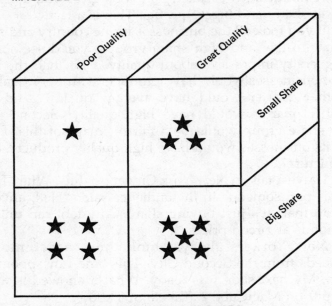

QUALITY AND MARKET SHARE

Kentucky they once built the LTDs. They used to call the plant the "war zone." Of all Ford plants it had the lowest quality rating. Its output was horrible. The workers just didn't give a damn.

"If something wasn't right, we'd let it go. . . . We didn't care a lot," said one assembler.[1]

Ford finally did something about it. They saw the light. Quality was becoming an industry-wide issue. The same plant down in Derbyland now makes Ford's most defect-free vehicles. It didn't just happen. Ford put a lot of high-paid executive time and big chunks of money into it. The company knew the quality strategy was worth it. They knew it would pay off. "Do you want to make a good

[1]Jeremy Main, "Ford's Drive for Quality," *Fortune*, April 18, 1983, p. 62.

16

product or do you want to shut down?" asked the plant manager.[2] It was as simple as that.

In one voice, the nation should be asking itself the same question. But that's a topic for the editorial page. For you, the message should be crystal clear. It's summarized in this Strateg-O-Gram:

BETTER QUALITY PAYS

If you have an ad agency, watch out. Don't let it, or anyone else gull you into backing away from quality. Stick to your guns. Accept no substitute for quality. Corner-cutting is tempting. And it can get to be a habit.

Do you know the term *creeping distortion?* Early hi-fidelity suffered from it. The system sounded great when you bought it. A few years later you noticed something was wrong. Eventually you couldn't stand listening to it. But the problem happened so gradually it wasn't notice-able at first.

The same creeping distortion can happen with any product or service. It happens with a little chiseling here, a little scrimping there. From one year to the next, consumers won't detect anything amiss. But suddenly the product simply doesn't deliver anymore. The aggregate quality decline can hurt sales and profits.

By the time you spot the damage, it may be too late. Your rivals will have made their move. So beware. There's always someone trying to score a few short-term brownie points. The microscopic cut-backs in quality they recommend make this an easy game to play. But the final minutes of the game bring declining market shares, and the score at the end is a lower ROI. Be stubborn, vigilant and defend your quality strategy. And if you haven't got quality, get it.

[2]Main, p. 63.

chapter six
But What Is It?

"I concur with everything you said, Link," announced
Squint. "The trouble is though, I'm not sure I understand
it."

T. Haller, *Link Dover at Harvard Business School*

Before embarking on your strategy mission, maybe you'd
like to know what quality is. Mostly, it's what you think it
is—excellence, performance, durability. It's stalwart,
stodgy stuff like that. But there's more.

Remember, this is business we're talking about here.
You have to pay the bills and still make a profit, so you
can't go hog wild. There is such a thing as too much quality. You wield quality competitively. You want to be *somewhat* better than your rivals. Enough to be noticed.
Enough to be appreciated. Enough to rise above that one-
shot mentality our ad agency buddies had.

Everybody probably has notions about what quality
entails. My father thought quality food had to be German.

My wife says it's French. I'd settle for a burger and fries. So in a sense quality is subjective. This makes some folks say you can't measure quality.

But these folks are wrong. We're not talking about an individual's notion of quality. We're talking about hundreds and thousands of people—the masses, the consumers. The quality we're talking about is in their eyes. What they think is more important than what you think. And certainly more relevant than anything your manufacturing or engineering people tell you about quality.

Now you could find out how consumers judge your quality (and we're talking here about the folks who actually use your product) by doing an expensive market survey. For example, you might ask which brand they liked best and why. This is how big companies judge quality perception. Big companies conclude they have high quality if consumers rated their product better than most of the others on the market. And vice versa.

I'm not saying you've got to do a survey, but you should talk to consumers. You'd be crazy not to. You'll be surprised how much you can find out. It doesn't take long to learn your standing in the quality sweepstakes.

If you want to improve your quality, look beyond the obvious. For example, beer is more than a golden liquid that tastes great and slakes thirst. Blindfolded, most people can't tell one brand from another. Yet they all have favorite brands they swear by. How come?

It all comes down to image, that's why. My ad agency pals go crazy over image. Even I have to admit it plays a role here. Image builds a quality impression in the user's mind.

Image can be used in several ways. Make consumers think your product is special. That you make it with great care and skill. That folks can enhance their reputation by using it. That their friends'll think they're richer, smarter, better bred, or whatever. Just by using your product.

Even industrial products have an image. You can't bury your head in the sand and hope it goes away. Otherwise it'll just develop on its own—like kudzu. And you won't like what you get. So pay attention to image. It's part of the baggage all products lug along with them.

Image influences how people perceive your quality. Perception's more important than a ringbinder full of spec sheets. So don't get carried away with physical traits and neglect the "imaginary" ones. If you do, you'll be tossing an incomplete quality pass.

My wife needs lessons in this. Last week, by mistake, she opened a can of potato soup. She cooked it and then said to the kids: "Do you want lunch. . . . It's just potato soup." Of course, they said they'd take a rain check, and ducked out the back door. I told her she should have said: "Hey, kids, you're in luck; I have prepared an exotic Hungarian festive soup with pepper seasoning. Come and get it while there's still some left." Knowing my kids, and how any chance for fake gourmandizing is met with rivalry over who gets seconds, they would have fought over the stuff. I can dupe those little perishers into eating anything with the right kind of image build-up.

You can't even afford to ignore your package. I don't care what you make or sell. The package is very important because it adds to your quality impression.

The brand name you give your product or service contributes as well. The look of your advertising, the kind of media you use, and the attitude of your salesforce all combine to produce your image.

All of these things are called the *marketing mix*. They should work together. If they do, they'll be greater than the sum of the parts. There's a name for this too. They call it *synergy*.

What it means is this: Extra mileage from a quality strategy by clever use of packaging, name, color, design and so on. Often it won't even cost extra. (You've got to have a package anyway, don't you?) You can make folks believe you've got greater quality than your competition, even when you don't spend more on it.

But all the parts must go together. Let's say you're selling the world's finest personal computer. And your TV commercials have "Star Wars" production values. What do you think customers will think if your reps wear polyester, diamond pinky rings, and white socks? Or if they chew on toothpicks when making their calls?

You have to function like a traffic cop. You must make certain every tactic locksteps with your quality strategy. It's self-defeating when they don't.

chapter seven
Why Quality Is Nice

"You make it too simple," complained Digby Bunkman.
"All business is simple," retorted Link, sizing up Bunkie
with a withering glance off the end of his patrician nose.
"Only simpletons look for complexities."
"Who're yuh calling a simpleton?" demanded Bunkman,
his jaw jutting forward aggressively.
"Sorry, old bean. Didn't mean it quite that way,"
apologized Link. "It's just that you pile on the bull feathers
and miss the obvious."

T. Haller, *Link Dover at Harvard Business School*

Joe Piscopo, as the loudmouth sportscaster, could sum up
this entire chapter without benefit of a single verb: "The
Big Connection. User attitudes. Sales. Bottom line: success; profits—very large."

I already chided the agency boys for their muddled
priorities. They liked to concentrate on getting folks to try
a product, but short-shrifted repeat sales. This is where
quality comes in. Quality gets you repeat sales. You already know this as a consumer. If a cunning commercial
sucked you into trying a new brand of toilet paper, would

you buy it a second time if it was as rough as sandpaper? Your customers are the same as you. Consumer perceptions of your product's quality govern whether they buy it, or not.

I like to tell the story about the time I got involved with dog food in France. (Yes, yes, I know, a funny thing to get involved with in that country.) In those days, the whole notion of dog food was newfangled to the French. It was a golden opportunity and three companies got into the act simultaneously. We thought we were going to teach French dogs a thing or two about haute cuisine. But, to be blunt, our product wasn't all that good. Blind tests (I'm serious) showed us that French dogs couldn't stand it. Recognizing this, we tried to inveigle management to improve the product's quality level.

"No way," said management. "This stuff's really selling. We just added a second shift." Better quality, we were told with artful Gallic metaphor, would be like gilding the lilly. Meaning, forget it.

Predictably, my story has a morbid ending. Nine months later our market share was sinking faster than mob squeelers in the Chicago River. As the market vaulted with hyper-growth, most dog owners were buying dog food for the first time. What did they know? They'd try all three brands once. But they'd only return to the brand their dogs enjoyed. Any dog lover would do as much. Once they learned their dogs wouldn't sit up and beg for our product, they stopped buying it. So when the market stopped growing, we ran out of new triers. That's what made our market share plummet.

No amount of advertising and marketing would have helped this situation. As a matter of fact, a business with poor quality products and very high marketing expenditures gets about the lowest ROI you can imagine. It's like flogging a dead horse.

If management had improved the quality, like I said, this wouldn't have happened. Not that I'm some kind of hero, it's just a well-established law of strategy. Quality assures continued business. In turn, continued business keeps your distributors and retailers happy. They are willing to do more for you, like giving you more prominent featuring and more shelf space. They take greater pains to avoid going out-of-stock on your product. And so on.

In some cases, product quality may even affect your company stock prices. The more security analysts read about technical problems on Coleco's Adam home computer, the closer they tracked it. They became gloomy about the company's prospects. Adam's problems even overshadowed Coleco's sensational "Cabbage Patch Doll."

In a funny kind of way, quality is the foundation of free enterprise. As Michael Novak explains in *The Spirit of Democratic Capitalism*, capitalism appeals to sinners, socialism to long-suffering saints. While there aren't too many saints, there are plenty of sinners. And sinners, by and large, want the pleasures only quality products (and vices) produce. The smart money is on the sinners. You can let the socialists have the saint market.

Declining quality can wreck a nation. The United State's situation today is similar to that of England. When England's quality standards slipped, it became a worldwide joke. I recall a BBC newscast covering a street riot in Ulster. In a single statement, the anchorman summed up the state of British craftsmanship when he said: "The police brought up the water cannon, but they failed to work." Younger readers, who associate Dudley Moore with towering Hollywood starlets and lame comedies, may be surprised to hear he was actually quite funny years ago. His Cambridge University review, "Beyond the Fringe," was the big hit on both sides of the Atlantic in the early 60s and derived much of its humor taking pot-shots at the loss of British workmanship. And in spite of all kinds of government programs, some spearheaded by a determined Prince Philip, nothing has changed. And now its happening here.

Quality isn't just uptight Puritan Ethic rectitude. It is the very soul of the successful business. High quality makes you the gentry of your industry. Quality gives you greater flexibility, more choices, more clout. It lets you raise prices without fear of losing too many customers, which gives you higher margins. It gives you more to spend on your advertising, which produces greater sales volumes. And so on and so forth—all the way to the bank.

I know you've studied Sun Tzu Wu's ancient bestseller, *The Art of War*. Remember where Wu said: "Rely not on the likelihood of the enemy's not coming, but on our own readiness to receive him; not on the chance of his not attacking, but rather on the fact that we have made our position unassailable." In plain Yankee, old Wu means keep your powder dry and your quality standards high. An unshakeable faith in quality comes as close as anything can to guaranteeing your survival. And as we said in Chapter 6, it delivers big profits.

Our Strateg-o-Gram is:

QUALITY BRINGS REPEAT SALES.

chapter eight
Being Different
for a Reason

It was a large dark room. In its center was a glass enclosure
illuminated by a single spotlight. What I saw made me sick.
A fat man, almost totally naked, was twisting and writhing
on a canvas mat. His hideous body was covered in tattoos.
                This guy was a damn mess.
          "Let's get the hell outa here!" I yelled.
     "No, you must watch him," my guide insisted.
The tattoos were changing. First there were green dragons,
then blue eagles. It changed to a moving hula-hula dancer.
You could see plenty of detail. Soon it showed scenes of
upcoming network shows. Mainly car chases. ABC-TV had
the most. Then red trickles oozed from the fat man's pores.
   "Will you ever forget him?" my guide wanted to know.
"Never! Let's get outa here fast!" I pleaded. After we left
     the room I asked what the point of all that was.
"The strategic law is one of differentiation. Our Tattooed
Man is so different no one ever forgets," he explained.

T. Haller, "Dr. Success"[1]

Friends often call me after losing their jobs. The first thing
they want to know is what it's like being in business for

---

[1]Terry Haller, *Dr. Success*, unpublished manuscript, 1984. Used with permission throughout.

yourself. Their tone usually gives them away. They want me to tell them self-employment is great, which I do if I'm in the mood. Then they unfurl their private yearnings.

"I'm gonna open up an office," they begin. "Be a consultant or something. I'm better than most of those yo-yos out there. What d'ya think?"

"Sounds super," I tell them. "But what's your marketing plan look like? I mean where's your unique selling proposition?" When you're a pro the jargon comes real easy. Usually they haven't got a marketing plan. They haven't thought about the mandatory accompaniment to quality we call *differentiation*.

Sure, they're all smart people. And I'd wager most of them *could* do a finer job than those they'd have to compete with. But, at the same time, most of my friends have only average sales ability. They'd have an uphill fight getting business unless they had some dazzling new benefit to offer their customers.

Differentiation has been a key underpinning of the quality strategy since folks first started living together in villages. The opposite of differentiation spells instant defeat and is known as being "me-too." Me-tooism often results from blind worship of the marketing concept. Here's what usually happens. Every firm in the industry discovers the same consumer needs. Soon they are all out there on the market trying to satisfy those same needs. In no time flat, the retail scene fills up with nearly identical products. Only the names are different.

Examples of differentiation are all about us. You could see the most glorious manifestation of unplanned differentiation by strolling through Chicago's neighborhoods. But be careful. Some of these neighborhoods you don't go into unless you're properly dressed—like wearing a live German shepherd around your neck. Suitably attired, you will see the greatest variety of food ever assembled. Wandering in from the lake a few blocks brings you face-to-face with plain old American, French, Italian, Greek, Mexican, Soul, Thai, Vietnamese, Chinese, Japanese, Jewish, and Arab restaurants. This mouth-watering differentiation entices food nuts to drive into neighborhoods so tough the cops will give you a ticket for not having a body in your trunk. Differentiation is a powerful magnet.

On the other hand, differentiation can get too fancy—just ask Detroit. It worked there when GM decided Henry Ford's "any color so long as it's black" edict was an opportunity to carve out a market segment. But over the years Detroit's differentiation got out of hand. In the 50s and 60s the VW Bug revived some of crusty old Henry's good sense. But it didn't catch on in Detroit. Differentiation proliferation just kept getting worse. Counting all its different permutations of engines, accessories, and gear shifts, the '84 Thunderbird offers customers 69,000 varieties.

Fans of the marketing concept will try to argue this is good for customers. But is it good for anybody when companies go through spells when they lose billions of dollars? The orgy of varieties and spinoffs pushes up the manufacturing cost. The average American car has over $1000 added to its overhead cost because of this.[2]

Still, a lot of folks think this is what marketing is all about. They must be wearing blinders. It does not make for a sound business at all. Significantly, few Japanese companies are guilty of excess differentiation. In fact, Japan's success may owe more to its limitations on models and varieties than to the legendary quality circles. Honda,

---

[2]John Koten, "Giving Buyers Wide Choices May Be Hurting Auto Makers," *Wall Street Journal*, December 15, 1983, p. 33.

for example, makes a mere 32 varieties available on its Accord automobile.

Here's why you must exercise restraint. Not only does limiting models let you sell your product at a lower price, it also lets you cultivate your quality strategy more vigorously. What you save by not having to tool up for different models, you can devote to quality improvements. Also, by concentrating bigger production runs on fewer models, you travel along the learning curve much faster. This, too, means lower costs.

Differentiation doesn't have to mean "plenty." It doesn't make any sense to go hog wild. An unending spate of models, colors, sizes, and accessories is the wrong type of differentiation. The right type of differentiation is more basic. It is your "reason for being." It is the justification you have for going into business, or for introducing a new product or service. The converse is being an "also ran." That seldom works. Me-too businesses don't deliver sparkling returns on their investments.

Differentiation is best viewed by how it applies to your product's basic thematic concept. If you have a well-founded concept, you should be a marketing success—all other things being equal. True, you miss out on some sales if you don't offer all possible varieties. But restraint lets you maximize your returns. For some reason, many marketing pros fail to grasp this. To be a good strategist, you must prevail on your marketing personnel to see the light.

Strateg-O-Gram:

DON'T BE ME-TOO. DIFFERENTIATE.

chapter nine
What Price Do I Set?

"Let's just lower our prices and get those sales up. That's
the ticket," said Bunkman.
"Hold on, old boy. Smokestack Flange has tough
competition with bigger shares and more cash. They'll
retaliate. Then where'll we be?" asked Link.

T. Haller, *Link Dover at Harvard Business School*

Price setting causes sleepless nights. We're judiciously
greedy. We don't want our prices so high they kill sales.
But another nightmare is setting our prices too low—and
later discovering consumers gladly would have paid more.
Any sane person wants top returns. Pricing is a potent
strategic weapon. But most people don't think that way.
Lazily, they just match their rival's price. That's seldom
wise.

There's an old story about the kid who was never
terribly bright in school. Years later an old buddy sees him
climbing out of a limousine and he asks how he managed
to get so rich. "I just buy and sell things, but I'm good at
pricing," he said. "But surely your margins must be aw-

fully high to have gotten so wealthy," his friend suggested. "Nope," he said, "Just one percent." "You mean you got rich on a mere one percent mark-up?" his friend inquired. "Yup, I buy stuff for a buck and sell it for two bucks."

Some pricing strategies may succeed without cerebral guidance. Most require analytical planning. A fact of life: market dominators get the highest prices. (Everything we said about the joys of big market shares applies here. No point going through all that again.) But few of us are market leaders. Let's say you are far from it. How then do you set your prices? Well, we already ruled out matching your competition's price. Parity pricing doesn't build market share (or sales volume).

That doesn't leave much choice does it? If you can't have the same price as your principal rival, then you've either got to be higher or lower, right? So what about a lower price? You could slash prices and give the market bully a real run for his money.

But let's think that one through for a minute. Price slashing could lead to a bigger problem. The big boy on the block isn't going to sit there cowering and letting you stomp all over him. Realistically, he can afford a longer price war than you can. His superior reputation (plus his bank of cash) will make him the easy victor.

And don't forget this: The leader has probably been using price-cutting to intimidate rivals since before you were born. It's a common practice to deploy price-cuts to dissuade newcomers from turf encroachment. (Sometimes market leaders don't even have to actually go through with it—it's enough for them to just threaten it.) The market leader might even enjoy a price war. To him it's pure rhapsody. Because if he wins, your share loss will be his gain. Do not underestimate his willingness to come down hard on you like a S.W.A.T. team. Do not push your luck. The market leader's objective will be to scare you off for good. For him fewer competitors is a lovely idea. It spells s-h-o-r-t-a-g-e and he can raise his prices even higher than before.

Having read all that, you're probably wondering why there are any discounters still in business. Think in terms of goals. You want a high return on your investment. Discounters survive—and in absolute terms rake in heaps of money—but in most industries they don't earn a high return. The volume potential has to be enormous for discounting to work. The one exception to this is in a commodity industry. The discounters here do fine because there is no other way to compete. A commodity market is essentially a price market.

But in most other kinds of industries discounters don't do that well. They have swollen working capital requirements. Even worse, unionization hurts discounters more than it does their regular-price cohorts. That's because union work rules strip away or hog tie cost controls basic to the health of a low-price strategy.

Well then, we've ruled out parity pricing and cut-pricing so that leaves us only one option: premium pricing. Some armchair strategists may tell you the easy road to wealth is going for a higher price than the market leader. Rather, it might lead to early retirement. Some very horrible things could be in store for you if you try it. Sure, you may enjoy those big margins for a few days. But the fun will end when your market share starts to slip. Since your market share is the way you master your costs, the long-run result is less profit, not more.

But don't get discouraged. There are some glimmering exceptions to this. If your imagination was animated by the last chapter, you're probably already thinking about it: differentiation. If your product is remarkably and desirably different from the competition, a higher price might work.

You have to handle this right though. It takes marketing virtuosity. Premium pricing a strongly differentiated article succeeds, as a general rule, when backed with heavy advertising. You can see why: differentiation is just an empty exercise if your customers don't cotton on to it or don't understand why it's better. Effective advertising gets your story across. It makes your customers gladly pay more.

To some the ultimate price weapon is the value strategy. This is the combination of quality and price. A

MAGICUBE 3

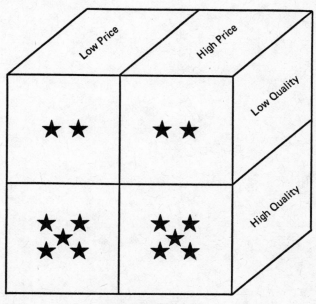

PRICE & QUALITY

high quality level with a low price would constitute high value. A MagiCube shows the relationship. Chapter 11 has more to say about value.

Strateg-O-Gram:

PRICING IS A STRATEGIC WEAPON.

chapter ten
Pricing New Products

"Come to think of it, when I first got sent up the river those little pocket calculators went for fifty bucks per. When I got out they were giving them away. I guess that's an example of the calculator folks using that crazy learning curve, eh?" I observed.

T. Haller, *Dr. Success*

In the old days, if your product was truly new and different, that is if you had no competition, you'd charge whatever the market would bear. But today's strategist would call that shortsighted. Your pricing policy on a new product will do a couple of things: promote sales (and market share) growth and elevate your margins. But it can only do one of these at a time.

Those who go for the highest price the market can stand are jumping the gun. They obviously haven't heard about the good old learning curve we talked about in Chapter 3. The learning curve makes your costs drop as production increases. Doing the same thing over and over makes even the dullest worker more efficient. The smart strategists learn to count on this. They know they will have a learning curve. So they set their prices at a point that gives them the profit margin they want at some future production level (where costs will be lower than they are at the outset). And they'll end up making more on the deal—much more than if they had succumbed to the initial temptation of high introductory prices.

This is how they make their markets grow, and how they discourage competition. (Some would-be competitors will be befuddled and wonder how they can make a profit and just give up.) Yeah, I know. This takes a lot of faith. And you're not sold. Some elaboration may be in order.

For one thing, it doesn't work on "new" products that are not strictly new but merely marketing repositionings or modifications. The sausage maker who decides to toss a different seasoning into his mixture and then touts it as "the new Schweinhundt brand of sausage," isn't going to have a learning curve.

For another thing, if it is a truly new product it's going to take your marketing folks a while to womp up demand. Thus, it is perfectly logical for you to ask: Why not go with a whopping high price at first but cut it the minute you detect competition fixing to come on stream?

The noble strategist hates compromises. Still this is an easier strategy to sell. It could attenuate your growth rate somewhat—maybe a whole lot; but sometimes it works by letting you pick off those more adventuresome consumers who will gladly bow to your high price for no other reason except your product is new. (As Barnum said, there's one born every minute.) Once you exhaust that sector of the population, you can deflate your price and pick up the cheapskates. One pleasant side-effect: a quality image may accrue from this procedure.

If you're not your own boss, and management is incapable of seeing the beauty of pre-learning-curve pricing, then this compromise may be the only approach you'd be able to sell. Politics is the art of the possible, after all. But while you're implementing this strategy, you should be tenaciously advancing the cause of using that learning curve. The faster you get your prices down, the more successful you'll be in repelling competition, and in seizing a dominant chunk of the market. All this will pay off in spades in later years.

Strateg-O-Gram:

USE THE LEARNING CURVE WHEN PRICING NEW PRODUCTS.

chapter eleven
Do I Have a Value for You

"I still say Smokestack Flange can meet foreign competition by slashing prices. That's my answer," proclaimed Digby Bunkman, all puffed up like a bullfrog.
"Not good enough, old buddy," responded Link Dover.
"But that's how the Japs do it," Bunkie shouted right back at him.
"Incomplete analysis, old sock. The Japanese also offer very high quality. That's what makes the difference," said Link.

T. Haller, *Link Dover at Harvard Business School*

While I've encamped in several different cities, my current abode has clear cultural advantages. Chief among them is the local revival cinema. For its annual Three Stooges Film Festival not only does it lower its ticket price, it also shows only the very best of these comedic classics. ("All with Curly" claims its advertising literature.)

That's what I mean by value: better quality at lower prices. If you're a Three Stooges fan, you'll know what I'm talking about. If, like my wife, you hate the Three Stooges, you will have to read the rest of this chapter.

Before we start let's reiterate two central points. Gen-

38

erally, low relative prices aren't terribly appealing to strategists. They don't give enough ROI to write home about. Conversely, high-priced differentiation often works quite well. But the catch is premium pricing requires skilled marketing, and that rules out a lot of business people—especially the technical genius sorts who don't have very good marketing instincts.

But what if you combined these two points? Suppose you said: "Okay, I'm small, and kind of a bust at advertising and marketing. But I put out a high quality item. So I'm going to forget about margins for a while. I'm going to buy the market. And I'll do it with a low price that doesn't chisel on quality. What I'll do will be to sell Tiffany quality at K-Mart prices." That, my good friend, is the value strategy. It usually works wonders—if ROI is what you had in mind.

Look, I'll say it just once more: Pricing can do two things for you. It can give you the margins you want (short-timers usually go for that). Or it can build share (this takes longer, naturally). And without something on the sexy side to back up a naked low-price strategy a share position doesn't endure for long—especially if you're a latecomer in the market. However, if you unleash the value strategy, you have a better shot at building share and keeping it—even if you arrived on the scene late in the game.

The quality component is your safeguard against the war-mongering market leader. He may be reluctant to enter into a price war with you now because you're not just justifying yourself to the consumer by a low price (as was the case back in Chapter 9). You've given the customer another reason to want to buy your product. The ballgame is now quite different.

Value is the strategy befitting the little guy. It lets a business with a small market share really hype its ROI. Its comparative gain is more dramatic than the big-share business. The big-share business will always have a higher ROI in the absolute, but its gain from following a value strategy isn't terribly impressive at all. MagiCube 4 shows this.

Strateg-O-Gram:

VALUE STRATEGIES GIVE LITTLE BUSINESSES A FIGHTING CHANCE.

MAGICUBE 4

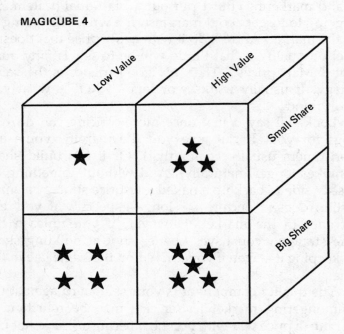

VALUE AND MARKET SHARE

chapter twelve
Growth Markets:
The Good & The Bad

We walked into the sales manager's office and sat down.
We didn't say a word. The sales manager sat at his desk
playing with his fingers. He would lock them together and
they'd battle each other. First, the right hand would seem
to be winning and then the left would overpower it. I didn't
get it at first. Then I noticed on one hand it said "Growth,"
the other "Hold."
"It just about sums up everything I know about strategy,"
the sales manager told us. Then he pressed the button of a
little black box sitting on his desk. In Porky Pig's voice the
box said: "Da dee, da dee, da dee, that's all folks."

T. Haller, *Dr. Success*

The morning Loopward-bound el ride is ideal for reading
the *Wall Street Journal*. Besides, early morning chats aren't
my style. So if I spot someone I know at the station I
usually duck out of sight—even if it's my broker friend.
The *Journal's* informational impact outweighs any com-
muting conversation I've ever had with this guy.

But I'm not always lucky and can't always duck him.
Take last month for example. Just as the train was pulling

out, he leaps on board, spots me, and sits down beside me. He opens his Murdockian *Sun-Times* from the back but soon tires of its rich diet of sporting news and asks me how my investment portfolio is doing.

"About the same," I tell him, breaking my train of thought and necessitating a reread of a sticky paragraph in the lead editorial of my *Wall Street Journal*.

"I've got something you'll be interested in," he says. Then he tells me about some small computer company whose stock his firm is obviously peddling.

"What's so great about it?" I mutter, half listening.

"Ground floor opportunity. A growth company in a growth industry. Now's the time," he tells me.

"What else?" I ask.

"What more do you need? Growth's enough," he says.

"Come on, this company isn't the only one in that vineyard. There must be hundreds," I reply.

"Sure, growth attracts everyone. Nobody wants to miss out," he says.

"But that's the problem," I explain. "They're already dropping like stars over Alabama. Video games, home computers, floppy discs—the industry's overloaded. The dead bodies are blighting the landscape of Silicon Valley." I was getting too poetic for him.

"You against computers or something? That's the future. Get with it," he grumbles, returning to the back pages of his *Sun-Times*.

If you ask the man-on-the-street, he'll tell you that growth markets are great. Anyone playing the market (and I don't mean only my broker pal) will choose growth industries hands down and shun the declining industries. If you're starting up your own business, you'd probably go into computers instead of buggy whips. It sounds like plain old horse sense—growth businesses are more attractive.

But growth also causes lots of heartburn. I'd even say this: More personal fortunes are lost in growth industries than in mature or declining industries. Sure, growth is nice for the nation. Unhappily though, for lots of business people, growth is like a snort of cocaine. It gives them a false rush of confidence. They make silly mistakes. They lose their shirts. All because they didn't follow the right strategies. Growth should be welcomed and embraced with a figurative hug, but treated like a menacing monster.

Random headlines from *Wall Street Journals* I managed to read on the el reveal the ominous side of the growth story:

> Market for robots turns sour, may speed industry shakeout (April 22, 1983, p. 21).
>
> Shakeout of Producers of Personal Computers Makes Buyers Nervous (November 25, 1983, page 1).
>
> Troubles at Mattel Seen Extending Beyond Fallout in Electronics Line (December 1, 1983, page 1).

Growing markets can attract both the wise (strategists) and the foolish (tacticians). The foolish outnumber the wise. Few new businesses succeed. Lots of reasons are summoned forth to explain the failure, but the main reason is that growth industries attract too many contenders. There simply isn't room for them all. And the failures are those who neglect to formulate the appropriate strategies for growth markets.

Growth is not only a monster, it's a hungry monster—hungry for cash. You need stacks of working capital. The more successful you are, the more working capital you need. Worse yet, your working capital needs grow monthly. That's because your accounts receivable and inventories keep growing in pace with growing sales.

Customers don't pay you immediately; and by the time they do pay up, your sales volume will once again have gotten bigger, and your working capital needs will be even larger.

A nice problem to have? No. Think ahead. Coming soon is that scary cycle mentioned in the headlines—the dreaded shakeout. That's when the market does something about its saturation problem. It's when the growth can no longer support all the contenders that it lured. The shakeout is the Big Accounting—the jolting judgment day when the heads roll. By now customers have sorted it all out. They elect which brand or companies they want around in the future. Distributors and retailers also decide whom they want to handle or stock. (In fairness, they can't handle them all.) Predictably, the trade won't display any fidelity to frail though determined weaklings with little real promise. The shakeout is a real bummer. (When my broker pal pushes a "growth stock" at me, my street instincts tell me the shakeout seeds may have already begun to sprout.)

Surviving the shakeout calls for early chest-beating aggressiveness. When the market is growing, you should push hot and heavy for massive sales and market share growth. It's easier to do this now than in a mature market (when it becomes nigh to impossible).

Plunging into a growth market in the right way means forgetting about showing a fast profit. You must be willing to invest cash and live with a lengthy negative cash flow. (Chapter 13 gives you the lowdown on cash flow.) This investment goes beyond recognizing that it'll take years to recoup your grubstake. You have to acknowledge that your returns may not even start for a number of years. Growth is one long drain. If you don't have the stomach for it—or if your bone-crusher boss demands immediate rewards—maybe you shouldn't get involved.

But noninvolvement is not actually a very suitable option. You can't go on forever in an ever-maturing market. Without some element of renaissance, all markets, sooner or later, die or experience deep transformations. Your long-term survival demands that you test your luck in growth markets at least occasionally.

I said your plunge into the growth market requires aggressiveness, but what does that really mean? Aggressiveness means spending big on marketing, sales, and advertising. Make your product known. Consumer or end-user awareness is the start of something great. Next, make customers believe you have superior quality and that your differentiation is compelling. Good consumer attitudes lead to repeat sales. The growth phase is the wrong time to skimp on the marketing effort. (Later, when the market growth abruptly vanishes like a wraith in the fog, you can cut back on the heavy marketing expenditures and relax.)

A point about product quality: In theory, quality in a growing market is less important than in a mature market because customers aren't very discerning. But remember that French dog food story I told in Chapter 7. Don't barge into a growth market with shoddy quality. Moreover, if you notice the standards of quality improving in the market, elevate your quality to keep ahead of the competition. That's also part of being aggressive.

Aggressiveness also means having more than enough production capacity. If you can't satisfy customer demand, your competitors will. In turn, that means you lose share. Share is always easy to lose, but hard to recover.

A word of caution is in order at this point. Don't bother being aggressively up-to-date on your plant and equipment. It would be a mistake to start out by installing a lot of costly ultramodern gizmos. It's too early for this. Growing markets encourage diverse technological advances, but their debugging takes time. Moving too fast could have you saddled with a factory full of obsolete junk. Adapt your old equipment, buy it used, or sign up co-packers and subcontractors to maintain capacity to serve the new growing market. Wait until the dust settles before investing heavily in hi-tech P&E.

You'll be able to tell if your aggressiveness has paid off when your business becomes one of the largest in the market. (In many industries, especially at the local level, you won't be able to get your hands on competitive sales data, but you will probably have a gut feeling that tells you if you've made it.)

In many large national industries there is a rough rule-of-thumb. It says that only the top three contenders will fetch a worthwhile ROI. The rest may as well put their money in a CD. Interestingly, the top three form a kind of pattern. The market share of the biggest will be about twice the size of the runner-up, and four times the size of the number three contender. I wouldn't say that's an unchangeable law, but it often works out that way.

Now, once you've managed to survive the dreaded shakeout, you should rein in your aggressiveness. But who ever admired a nonaggressive business person? Aggressiveness is adulated by the common folk in the business arena. I can sympathize with anyone who is hesitant to give it up, but you have to wake up and smell the Folgers. The market has levelled off. The rapid growth is gone, probably forever. If you continue being aggressive, you're never going to have a chance to build back those cash reserves you depleted getting your huge market share. If you can't manage to throttle the aggressive urge now, the whole battle will have been in vain. By seeking the benefits of honeyed peacefulness, you're not being a wimp—you're just being smart.

This doesn't mean you have to drop off to sleep. But it is the signal for a new game plan. Your marketing efforts must now become defensive. Your days on the offensive squad are over. If this is against your nature (it drives some people nuts) then get a reassignment. The business needs a positive cash flow. Don't stand in the way.

Strateg-O-Gram:

GROWTH MARKETS DRAIN CASH, END IN SHAKEOUT. AGGRESSIVE MARKETING NECESSARY.

chapter thirteen
DUH Take

"First, we gotta set our goal," said Link.
"No sweat," said Squint, "Smokestack's goal is a fat profit."
"Falderal," asserted Mary Moneyham. "Profit is accounting subterfuge that dupes dummies like you. Mafia bookkeeping is better. Just find out what the take is."
"I think she means cash flow, men. And by golly, she's right," beamed Link.

T. Haller, *Link Dover at Harvard Business School*

Actually, this chapter's got nothing to do with strategy. Instead, it's about cash flow. If you aren't too sure what cash flow is (and why it's crucial) you may want to invest a few minutes in reading this chapter.

Cash flow is commonly defined as profit plus depreciation, but that's not very exact. A better way of looking at cash flow is that it's the difference between all the cash coming in and all the cash going out. Cash flow, in other words, is just what it sounds like. Don't search for something mysterious.

For a number of reasons, cash flow is more important

than reported profits. The problem with profit is that it's basically a function of taxation regulations. Since the IRS has complicated everything so much, profit can be figured in several different ways. Consequently, "profit" doesn't really give you a true picture of how well a business is doing. Profit, as shown in a company's P&L Statement, is not an absolute. It's a compromise between wanting to show a high profit to tickle the shareholders, and a low profit to lighten the tax burden.

If you have an accounting background, you probably don't want to know more. But for the curious, here are two examples: One is how depreciation is treated. Depreciation schedules don't affect cash flow, but they're diverse enough to lend accountants tremendous flexibility in playing with reported profits. Inventory evaluation is the other example. Whether you use LIFO or FIFO makes no difference on your flow of cash, but it does alter what you show as profit. Get the problem?

Cash flow represents the unpadded truth. Focusing on cash flow lets you avoid all these misleading wiggles. Don't ask me why it receives insufficient emphasis in financial circles. That would open a nasty can of worms that'd be the subject for another book.

(Before I forget, I should mention that when I talk about ROI in this book I'm using operating profit, which is a little purer than net profit. More to the point, my strategy laws and the MagiCubes would come out the same if we used cash flow instead.)

Okay, now let's relate this to strategy. As I started to say in the last chapter, big market shares usually deliver positive cash flows once the market growth rate slows down. Small market shares seldom give you a positive cash flow (unless you're on the far end of a triumphant learning curve). Growth markets don't spout cash either. They require cash infusions to keep up with the growth.

Cash flow is one more reason why the name of the game is market share. And it's why I said you should aggressively build share in a growing market, but not in a mature market. In mature markets (assuming you have succeeded in building a decent share), you can start enjoying the fruits of your labor: a positive cash flow. In fact, that's probably the only time you're going to have such a chance.

So that's the thrilling story of cash flow. Unfortunately, we're not through yet. Here's something else to complicate your life a bit further.

Have you heard of *discounting*, as in the famous phrase "discounted cash flow"? Maybe your personal computer keeps showing something it calls "DCF" and you wondered what it was. Discounting is like backwards interest rates. It is used to figure out the true value of a future stream of cash flow, taking into account the havoc of inflation and financing costs. Discounting is really the best way to assess a future cash flow, but most business people don't bother, even when computers can do all the work. Maybe that's because most business people are secretly confused by it.

If you're still curious, here's an example: Suppose two different companies, A and B, want to hire you to do a three-year project. Company A will pay you $90,000 in advance. Company B will pay $100,000 when you finish the job. Assume 10% annual inflation and 10% interest rates. The question is which is the sweeter deal? The answer is company A's advance payment of $90,000. The reason why is because you can invest the $90,000 at 10% a year which'll wash out the 10% inflation. So at the end of three years you'll have $90,000 in purchasing power.

On the other hand, the $100,000 you'd get from Company B at the end of three years would have shrunk in purchasing power because of inflation. It's real value would be only $73,000 then. It'd drop 10% in the first year leaving $90,000, by the end of year two it'd be down to $81,000, and by the end of the third year you'd only have $73,000 in buying power—and that's not even taking into consideration the opportunity cost of not being able to use the dough sooner.

Well, that's the concept of discounting. I cleaned it up by omitting tax consideration and a few other quirks, but that's the rough idea. If you need to know more, you can talk to an accountant.

Now, back to our continuing saga of business strategy.

chapter fourteen
The New Product

"Let's hire idea men. Get 'em to dream up hot new products," advised Bunkman lurching forward in his chair. "Not so fast, Bunkie. We're under-capitalized. The heavyweights will first toy with us like cats with a mouse. Then they'll pounce," cautioned Link.

T. Haller, *Link Dover at Harvard Business School*

There's a tribe in New Guinea that believes their god is a swivel chair. It seems many years ago the colonial governor sat in one. He was the closest these bushdevils ever got to a real god. When his regime collapsed, the governor took a fast hike, forgetting his chair behind him. And one thing led to another.

In the business world, we're more with it than that. We think God is a new product. We have proof, too. We can point to nations like England that ducked out of the new product worship service once too often. It was then that the English began learning the meaning of the word "wrath."

Perhaps you believe this. Maybe you think new

products might be good for your economic health. Maybe you've maximized your sales potential and see new products as the only logical route to greater volume. You may be right. Then again, maybe not. There are maps to follow on your new product journey.

The two most obvious laws on new product strategy come from ancient China: "Mouse with but one hole is easily taken." "Do not throw stone at mouse and break precious vase." Translation into English: You're safer from competitive threats when all your eggs aren't in the same carton. And don't let new products detract you from the old lines that are supplying them with the cash.

For any business that hopes to be around for a while, new products are unavoidable. Hank Ibsen, the playwright, once said: "I hold the man is in the right who is most closely in league with the future." In fact, the romance of business, from the silk-and-spice trade down to the present, is the story of obsolescence and innovation. Falling behind isn't good for the career. Not having the guts to make long-term commitments isn't good for the corporation.

This doesn't mean keeping up is a picnic. New products are risky. Blunders abound, and easily outnumber the success stories. In the food business, for example, you're lucky if more than 2% of your new products make it. Good strategies reduce the risk, however.

What exactly do we mean by new products? A new product is similar to pornography. I mean, you know it when you see it, but can't define it. I'd say just about anything with a novel principal feature is new. Even a toothpaste boasting a new flavor would count. Some companies will count new package sizes. It's probably a new product if you think it is. When Procter & Gamble came out with the Duncan Hines Chocolate Chip Cookie they called it a new product—even though the chocolate chip cookie had been around for eons. The justification for this was a new patented baking process that made P&G's cookie different: It gave the product an outside crispness but an inside chewyness (or a "plurality of textures" as P&G describes it). That made it new.

What we call "high tech" is another chapter in the new product annals. Those who think high tech is a whole new kind of animal may find themselves out in left field. Merely because a thing harbors microchips or fiddled genes doesn't mean it follows new rules. In terms of strategy, nothing has changed.

While new products tactics are fun to work on, you've got to keep your mind on half a dozen pivotal strategic issues. The first of these strategic issues is market share. Remember your marketing objective is to grab as big a market share as possible. A tiny share won't give you enough cash flow to make it pay out.

The second strategic issue is to protect your rear. Allow yourself to be haunted by that old adage: The pioneers are the ones with arrows in their backs. New products attract flocks of imitators. Then cometh ye olde shakeout to blow them all away—except for the scramblers who reached, and held, the mountain top. If you smell a shakeout heading in your direction and lack the resources to stave it off, you may be better off selling out while you've still got assets worth selling.

A few clever pioneers manage to prolong life by keeping a tight lip about their astounding success. That's hard to do with so much available data floating around these days. It's especially hard to keep the experts in conglomerate business development offices from knowing of your success. But keeping quiet might work for you—especially in small local markets or unconcentrated industries.

The third strategic issue is knowing when the market has reached its "newness threshold." When a market grows 10% or more per year, you're usually talking new products. But if fast growth persists for a few years, you may think the product has lost its newness. You may be then agitated by a temptation to develop something even newer than new. Take care because the thing to recognize here is that growth markets don't eagerly embrace another layer of "new" products. It's overkill, not unlike an interior decorator trying to make a Vegas casino look plusher. Wait until the time is right, which is after the growth rate peaks. New products work best in mature markets. They're often the shot in the arm a stodgy market needs.

The fourth strategic issue is your size. New products are a special boon to the small-share business. A serious new-product commitment could double its ROI. While that still won't give it an ROI as big as its high-share rivals, a doubled ROI is better than a poke in the eye with a sharp stick.

Big-share businesses actually don't derive enhanced jollies in their ROIs from their new product activities. But that's not the fault of new product strategies. It's because they already have whopping big ROIs. It's hard to go much higher.

The fifth strategic issue is the breadth of your line. Regardless of your market share, if a new product serves to broaden your line it could be beneficial. The business with a very broad line will always have the larger ROI.

The final strategic issue is timing. The question I'm asked most about new products concerns latecomers. What happens, I'm asked, if the market already got going before you put your act together? Can a latecomer make any headway? The answer is if you're just an average me-tooer, it's too late to bother.

But there is a way for a latecomer to get in on the

action. I covered most of the story on value in Chapter 11. But one further thing about the value strategy is that it gives a lift to the tardy who wish to deploy a new product strategy. MagiCube 5 shows this.

MAGICUBE 5

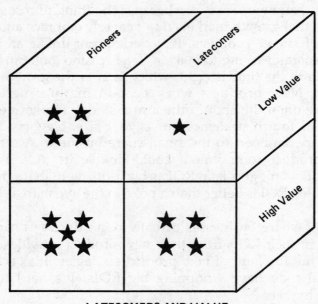

LATECOMERS AND VALUE

chapter fifteen
R&D

"Smokestack Flange needs a research unit. Yeah, that's it.
Test tubes, retort stands, the spark machines and flashing
lights. Like in the Frankenstein movies," proclaimed
Squint, waxing enthusiastic.
"Labs aren't like that anymore," corrected Mary.
"Don't even need one," said Link. "R&D doesn't fit here at
all."

T. Haller, *Link Dover at Harvard Business School*

New products and improved products start with an idea.
Ideas sometimes come from the funniest places. Before
Frank Baum wrote "The Wizard of Oz," he told his story
to his kids. They asked him what this funny country was
called. Baum tried to think up a name for it. Staring off in
space, he noticed his filing cabinet. It had two drawers.
One was marked "A-N," the other "O-Z." So that's
where the now famous name came from.

The spark of inspiration, the really great ideas, don't
come to people sternly applying themselves. Being tied to
a desk, computer console, or lab bench doesn't cut it.
Ideas can't be forced.

Back in the nineteenth century, an Austrian chemist, Friedrich von Stradonitz, was trying to figure out the molecular structure of benzene. Getting nowhere, he said forget it and took a nap. He dreamed of a snake with its tail in its mouth. This led to his accurate determination that benzene's atoms form a circle.

There are many stories like that. The brandname "Ivory" didn't occur to Harley Procter at work. He heard the word in a Sunday sermon. The Ivory soap bar floats because a worker forgot and left the mixer running over his lunch hour. It's called serendipity.

Do you really need an R&D department? Well, obviously if your product is technology-dependent you can't escape it. Ideas require structure and implementation. But the correct question is how much R&D and under what circumstances?

The key to the problem is size. Bigness and R&D go well together. Smallness and R&D do not. The logic of this is simple. Big companies get more ROI gain out of their R&D functions because they have more money. They can afford better lab equipment. They can afford to hire better people. They keep them happier longer because of their superior lab equipment, and accordingly get better work out of them. All of this is bound to lead to something and that something is usually interesting new products and more efficient manufacturing processes.

Small companies can rarely match this (though sometimes when begun and run by resplendent R&D types they manage for a while). The odds are against the small company ever getting much mileage out of its R&D department. When their R&D effort does hit pay dirt, the bigger companies quickly copy and out-market them.

Having big market shares also heightens the worth of R&D. That's because big market shares and marketing savvy go hand-in-hand. And it takes marketing savvy to turn R&D ideas into profitable products. High R&D expenditures backfire with the low-share SBU. In fact, the more it squanders on R&D, the lower it's ROI goes. MagiCube 6 shows this.

MAGICUBE 6

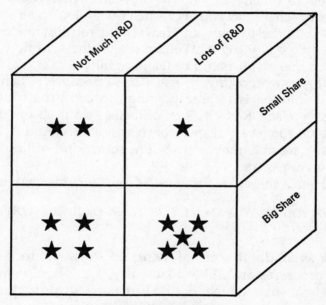

R&D AND MARKET SHARE

Making R&D work also takes a fairly high level of vertical integration (discussed more fully in Chapter 17). That makes sense when you think about it. A business with low vertical integration doesn't really do much. One example would be an assembly-type of operation that buys all its components on the outside. What would it need R&D for—unless it specifies custom-made components? Conversely, the business that is highly integrated has all kinds of things it can apply its R&D talents to.

The Strateg-O-Gram is:

KEEP R&D MODEST UNLESS YOU ARE BIG.

So where does that leave you if your business doesn't happen to qualify as big? Be honest, when you wrote exams in school did you ever—just once—look over someone's shoulder to copy an answer? It probably made you feel a little guilty, right? Well, in the business world copying can make you rich, not feeling guilty.

If you're too tiny to use R&D effectively, then the logical solution is (where possible) to copy the fruits of someone else's R&D. Knock-off artists do it all the time, but so do some very respectable corporations. And if copying isn't feasible maybe wangling some kind of licensing deal would work.

Hence the other Strateg-O-Gram for this chapter is:

IF YOU'RE TOO SMALL FOR YOUR OWN R&D, TRY COPYING INSTEAD.

Being small doesn't mean giving up. New products and new processes are still available if you dig hard enough. There's always someone who'll make a deal; frequently they are to be found overseas. If you've never thought that the time has come for America to renew its national commitment to R&D and new products just watch the old Bond movie, "Casino Royale," the next time it's on the Late Show. As usual, before he sets out to save the planet, Bond goes to his headquarters to get outfitted in the latest spy gadgets. One of them is a wrist-TV. Since the movie was made in 1967, Bond is very impressed by this item and asks who invented it. The head bloke says: "The Americans came up with it, actually." This is the funniest line in the whole movie. But it's also sad. It hits home harder than all the news shows warning us of our impending technological doom.

chapter sixteen
Segmenting Onward

It was more like a giant church than a meeting hall. The elevator dumped us at one end and I could hardly see the other end. The lighting was real spooky. Mostly, the place was dark, but shafts of light came down from the ceiling, ending in circles on the floor. Way up in the front, marble steps led to a stark white altar over which a flashing neon sign said: KNOW THY MARKET SEGMENTS.

T. Haller, *Dr. Success*

A brief word about market segmentation. To casual observers, the market for a given product looks quite unified. They think breakfast cereals, to cite one example, are one product category occupying a single market. But to the segment-minded sophisticate, breakfast cereals do not represent a monolithic market. Even consumers don't treat them that way. In fact, breakfast cereals break down into five distinct market segments, each segment capable of having totally different strategic problems and opportunities. These five segments are: (1) old-fashioned, hot, cooked cereals such as Cream of Wheat; (2) the more modern instant hot cereals, such as Instant Quaker Oats; (3) the standard ready-to-eat cold products, such as Corn Flakes; (4) the presweetened ready-to-eats, like Sugar Frosted Flakes; and (5) the natural or health-oriented cereals such as Quaker 100% Natural Cereal.

While segmentation sounds like more of that latter day, tedious business-school jargon, market segments are hardly new. The strategic thinking on them is quite new, however. The most important thought is that segments behave like separate, monolithic markets. Because of this you must learn to identify them for your industry in order to formulate victorious strategies.

By the way, it's no accident that this chapter follows the chapters on new products because an innocent new product introduction is often the coital beginning of the birth of the new market segment. (You can tell a new segment is aborning when competitors join the fray and their combined growth rate leaps into the 10%-plus ballpark.) When a new segment rises up from the muck of an established market, you have all the familiar strategic laws of the market to consider: the primacy of market share within the new segment, the judicious application of your learning curve, and so on. The segment may be new, but the strategies aren't. Market segments can develop and grow anytime, anywhere. It doesn't always require new technology.

The acetaminophen market segment is an example of what happens when a company ignores the development of a new market segment. Acetaminophens have been around for 25 years or more, but not until Johnson & Johnson's 1975 ad campaign for Tylenol did they really zoom. Millions switched from aspirin to acetaminophen, most of them going to Tylenol. (Tylenol was the innocent vehicle for some puzzling murders a few years back, but

J&J managed to cure that headache with yeomanly marketing and PR efforts.) Meanwhile, Sterling Drug, makers of Bayer Aspirin, the "aspirin" segment leader, elected not to plunge into this new segment. Maybe they thought such a move would hurt Bayer Aspirin sales, so instead they let Tylenol do the hurting.

Remorsefully, seven years later, the Bayer folks amended their thinking and brought their overseas Panadol acetaminophen to the United States. "We're going fishing where the fishing's best—to Tylenol customers," said a Sterling executive at the time. But the history of strategic studies teaches us it is not easy to catch up with a market leader, like Tylenol, with everything strategically going for it. As J&J discovered, the creation of a new segment can turn out to be an artful end-run around a dominant competitor in the dormant or declining market. But J&J wasn't the first to discover this: Volkeswagon did it in the 1960s, and designer jeans in the 1970s. In fact, the segmentation end-run has been a common economic occurrence for centuries.

Market segmentation is often thought of as a strategy. It isn't. In itself it is not a cause of your ROI performance, but it is an environment for strategy. Strategies are played out at the segment level, and only at that level. You must therefore learn to recognize them and formulate all your business strategies in that context.

The relevant Strateg-O-Gram is:

ALWAYS FORMULATE STRATEGY AT THE SEGMENT LEVEL.

chapter seventeen
Manufacturing Strategy

"I'm dying to meet the production workers. I mean, they're
so down to earth," bubbled Squint, mounting the chartered
bus that would cart the Production Class to a local shoe
factory for a field trip.
"They're gonna love my advice about quality circles,"
added Digby Bunkman with sublime confidence.

T. Haller, *Link Dover at Harvard Business School*

Yankee know-how. What ever happened to it? That kind
of thing never stays around long. In the 1600s, the Dutch
locked up the world's cloth trade, but the British, discovering more efficient manufacturing methods, seized market
leadership a hundred years later. By the early 1900s, textile
leadership had yielded to the Japanese, who have since
lost it to their Asian neighbors. Most industries follow
such a pattern.

The faltering efficiencies of our factories have been
given a shove by the prodigal demands of our marketing
people. Their reverence for the marketing concept forced
our manufacturing people to gear up for more product

variations than their productive facilities could handle efficiently. When you reflect on the comparison between the Thunderbird's 69,000 potential variations and Honda's 32, you have some idea of the astounding dimensions of the problem.

Whatever it is you do as a nation, if you can't do it well enough to compete in the world marketplace, you simply have to stop doing it. Not abruptly maybe, but eventually. And that's precisely what's happening in the United States. During the 1970s, this nation created 19 million new jobs, but 87% of them were service jobs, not manufacturing.

The plain fact is this country has to export in order to survive. We can export our services to some extent, which mainly comes down to exporting technology. Technology is easy to steal or copy. Before long any nation that needs technology in large enough quantities starts making it itself. (One shuddering thought: Soon even the menial aspects of computer jockeying will be handled off-shore, and relayed back to the United States via satellite. There are a million English-speaking clerks in Calcutta anxious to do it at very attractive rates.)

Those luncheon speakers who "face the future with confidence and optimism" tell us eventually all our plants will be retrofitted to match our high-tech needs. But for the more realistic among us meanwhile, there is much we can do to improve the productivity of even our moat-and-drawbridge factories without going robot-crazy.

In the first place, many of our factories are too big. I know this is a surprising statement. We used to think that the big plant would be more efficient. But it turns out not to be the case. A big anything takes "teamwork." That's a nice sounding word. But let's be realistic. Teamwork exists only when nobody feels a compulsion to cover his or her ass. In most organizations true teamwork seldom exists. (Though it can appear to exist for those naturally endowed with leadership traits: they get to be team captains.)

Gigantic plants reach a choke-point of human interaction that just encourages snafus. You get political infighting, buck-passing, and plain old managerial screw-ups. Some companies, such as 3-M for instance, are splitting things into smaller units of 100 souls, or so. Smaller outfits are easier to control. Small means managers can visualize the whole shooting match in their mind's eye. Small means they can make better snap, down-on-the-line judgments. Small gives managers greater flexibility so they can bounce back faster from economic adversity. Conversely, the humunguous plant is like a busload of snoozing passengers stuck in the mud.

This brings us to the point in the book where we have to discuss vertical integration. It's an issue that has to be treated with great care when seeking better manufacturing strategies. An example of vertical integration is the Hong Kong tailor in the following story.

A gentleman visits his tailor in Hong Kong and tells him he requires a very special suit—he's getting married. The Hong Kong tailor tells him he will make him the very best quality suit for such an auspicious occasion. The tailor explains that he has his own sheep ranch in Australia. He'll go there and select the choicest lambs and set them apart for special feeding and grooming. When their wool is sheared he will select the finest bales and ship them to the Chinese mainland, where that nation's best female hand-loomers, after receiving a training program on London's fashionable Bond Street, will loom the cloth with such care it will be suitable for an English lord. Then, he, the famous tailor, will himself measure, cut, and fit the suit. He will provide a total of ten fittings so that not even the slightest tailoring defect will be tolerated. And when the Hong Kong tailor had thus completed his sales pitch the customer said: "But I'm getting married at noon tomorrow."

"No problem," said the famous Hong Kong tailor, "Will have suit for you this afternoon."

Many manufacturing executives assume the proper strategy for getting higher plant productivity is having greater vertical integration. There are times when this kind of thinking can be disastrous. Upping your vertical integration level only works well when you have a big market share. If you have a small share, you simply don't have a decent learning curve. This means you'll never extract much gain from all the extra plant and equipment you have to invest in. The big share/high vertical integration combo also brings an additional boon: It permits you to draw more ROI mileage out of your R&D. As we said before, if you have a low vertical integration level there isn't a whole lot to apply your R&D to as a general rule. MagiCube 7 illustrates on this.

Some low integration businesses think they can spend their way out of trouble with added marketing clout, which is wrong. They simply don't have enough control over the entire productive process—they can't control their suppliers. The added burden of high marketing costs often brings their ROIs down to our one-star level.

You can't have a serious discussion about manufacturing without someone complaining about unions. Most plant managers would gladly do away with labor unions. Perhaps, if current trends persist, the unions may do away with themselves. Although unions aren't always that big a drag on ROI. If you're in management, you may think unions are a pain. (They, of course, think you are too.) But the facts show that unions only hurt the ROIs of big-share

MAGICUBE 7

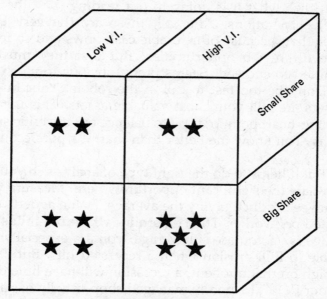

**VERTICAL INTEGRATION
AND MARKET SHARE**

businesses. That's right—with small-share businesses unionization has little or no ROI impact. Here's why: It's through work rules, not wage rates, that unions inflict the greatest harm. The small-share shop is usually a loose one with excess capacity. In contrast, the big-share business is tightly structured, with little slack, such that minor snags in work flow result in all kinds of trouble. When work-rule induced snags slow up production, out-of-stock conditions develop causing lost sales and depressed market shares. A company that loses market share must subsequently spend heavily to regain it. Down goes its ROI. Unionization in a big-share firm moves the ROI from the five-star to the four-star quadrant in a MagiCube.

We can, I suppose, hope that one day organized labor will realize what it is doing to our leading (i.e., the big-share) corporations. After all, these are the very businesses that, because of favorable cash flows and so forth, create future job opportunities. But first they must be permitted to succeed. Seems pretty obvious to me.

Don't be too fast to call in the robots. Your human workers are still your most valuable assets. This is not a bleeding-heart point of view to balance out my criticism of unions. You know me better than that. It's pure economics.

But it helps to do the right type of analysis so you can appreciate the significant opportunity here. Measure your employee productivity by the average "value added" contributed per worker. Then determine what your industry's average is. If you are subaverage, you are especially vulnerable to ROI erosion when a recession hits. But if you are high on that quotient, a recession will have little drain on your ROI. The poorly managed shop usually has a low value-added-per-worker quotient. It's usually ill-fitted to avert declining efficiency when slowdowns occur. It has negligible cerebral guidance. It comes unstuck under pressure.

A gargantuan high-tech investment obviously will raise the investment factor in the ROI equation. Yet it is commonly assumed that the bigger the investment (assumed today to mean high-tech stuff), the bigger the returns. Sadly, bigger returns are almost never the case when investment outstrips the worker-value-added quotient. Too many businesses are unaware of this. They expect high-tech wonders to transport them to the never-never land of hyped ROI. It won't happen without the human element.

One reason for this is the management clutch response. The added investment makes managers look awful when they have excess capacity on all that costly new equipment. Not only does it lower their ROIs, it makes them look like incompetents. So they will try anything to avoid P&E underutilization. Desperation leads to some pretty stupid moves. Their decision-making apparatus malfunctions. They get flop sweat. For example, they won't bargain hard enough with their suppliers out of fear of provoking halts in the flow of materials. So they end up paying more than they normally would have. These same managers will sit at the bargaining table, across from the union representatives, with their hats in their hands, almost eager to sign off on a generous settlement just to avoid a strike that would lower output further. Some managers in such a bind will slash all the discretionary items in their budgets—like advertising expenses and sales force travel allowances. Naturally, this leads to further sales erosion and things just get worse. And it all came about because someone had to get fancy with a showplace high-tech factory. Look before you leap. Elevate that worker-value-added quotient before you do anything you may later regret.

Another quotient to watch is asset productivity: the ratio of dedicated assets to your value added. It should be kept fairly low. Low would be in the 0.8 ballpark, high would be over 1.1.

And, finally, one more quotient to fuss about is the ratio of assets to employee; i.e., how much you have invested per worker. Industries vary too much to offer a suggested ideal figure. You could make industrywide comparisons on your own, and you should also plot your internal trends to make sure this quotient isn't getting out of hand.

When the previously mentioned two (asset productivity and assets per worker) quotients are carefully controlled in tandem, they can advance the ROI of your business significantly. The message again is that the mere act of investing in fancy P&E won't raise your ROI much until you make these assets work hard and smart. High tech brings no guarantee of enhanced profitability. If your value added per employee is high only because your per employee asset commitment is also high, you haven't got such a hot deal. The lazy investment in P&E gives you increasingly lower returns regardless of how high your investment intensity per worker grows. The energetic investment in P&E gives you tremendous leverage against all adversities, including unions and recessions.

Don't get upset if you find this to be a bit complicated. Most readers do at first—but that's no excuse to ignore it: It's the major reason why many analysts claim that America's most serious industrial problem is overinvestment.

Here's a blatantly simple-minded illustration that may uncomplicate it for you. An office has been doing the same kind of steno work for the past 50 years. In the beginning they used old-fashioned manual typewriters. Thirty years ago they replaced them with electric typewriters. Then, recently, they installed word processors. Strangely, productivity stayed the same: a typing speed of 60 words-per-minute and a daily output of around 45 pages. How come? They've increased the average asset investment per employee, and they've made the big move to high tech. So what gives? Peer group pressure and lousy people management is the answer. Over the years, the typists' office culture has ordained that 60 words-per-minute is the acceptable speed and 45 pages a day is a decent day's work. Woe betide the typist who transgresses against group norms. Management would be advised in this case to install incentive programs to improve the typists' value added output. With word processors this would be easy to implement since performance records are easy to obtain.

The central message of this chapter is that, in America today, one of the worst problems is the spendthrift habit of making ever bigger investments with ever lowered asset efficiency. The yield trend is toward lower ROIs. As a first step, harder working assets are needed in many industries, not more automation. This is the key manufacturing strategy to pursue.

The Strateg-O-Gram is:

MAKE ASSETS WORK HARDER BEFORE DECIDING TO AUTOMATE.

chapter eighteen
Financial Strategy

"Finance? Oh, that's simple," said Bunkman, his lower lip
protruding like Cheetah's, "It's all about stocks and bonds
and a few other things."

T. Haller, *Link Dover at Harvard Business School*

"High finance." The words alone conjure up visions of
oak-panelled boardrooms, plush carpeting, and billion
dollar deals sealed with a handshake. High finance pro-
vides gripping news items for the daily paper and insider
gossip for moguls and traders. It all sounds like the most
momentous thing happening in the world: Men in well-
cut, real wool suits, their teeth clamped on five dollar
cigars, calling the shots that activate the engines of mighty
industries. But it's all just a lot of horse feathers.

The only important thing about finance to the
strategist is how to control investment intensity. All the
rest is mechanics and instruments—none of which contributes to the enhancement of the economic value of the
corporation. Oh sure, they may stir up a short-term com-

motion on the stock market, but the long-run impact on share prices is dependent on cash flow (a controversial point but I'm sure it's right) and that is a product of your business strategies. (More on this in Chapter 22.) The particular strategic focus in finance should be almost exclusively on investment intensity because that's where the problems and opportunities are found.

Lamentably, slews of businesspeople don't have any idea how to decide whether to make a capital investment. Their approach to the capital outlay ranges from primitive to simplistic. Some choose to determine an investment's desirability by its likely impact on sales volume. Others calculate its impact on market share. Neither approach, unfortunately, relates to the size of said investment.

Some calculate the investment's payout—the number of years it'll take to get the investment back. That's better, but somewhat crude. In the more sophisticated companies you'll find people making a forecast of the investment's ROI, or even better of its cash flow (discounted of course).

Though it may seem that, once again, we've strayed from our subject, investment intensity is something all strategists have to worry about and it's wise to know exactly how to worry about it. The good strategist will watch for signs of overinvestment. Grade Four math will show that as capital intensity rises (assets/sales) your ROI will tumble. Contrary to popular belief, the heavy investment is not often the most profitable.

A related warning: Watch out for slipping leverage. Does each incremental dollar invested produce more or less ROI? Many operations foresake leverage as they retrofit their surplus or neglected assets with little hook-ons rendering them capable of earning a decent return in the context of the often used argument that "the original asset had no (book) value." I've seen entire corporations puff themselves up into a fairly high-volume enterprise on such an opportunity-cost philosophy. The results are criminal. They end up with a one-star level of ROI. It's a subtle process. The average manager never sees it happening until it's too late. Opportunity-cost thinking always sounds fine at the time, but it soon gets to be a habit. Then the entire operation becomes marginal. It is up to the strategist to prevent the cycle from beginning in the first place.

The strategist should also know what to do about flushing out the analytical distortions caused by inflation. He or she may demand that replacement value accounting be used to put the ROIs of different SBUs on an equal footing. If the relevant assets were acquired at different times over a number of years the failure to employ replacement value might have a sick influence on corporate thinking. Since any asset you buy today will have a higher dollar value than the book value of your older assets, it's always going to look like a bad investment (i.e., it's bound to have a lower ROI). It could make the company want to hang on to its assets long after they outlive their usefulness. As I cautioned in the last chapter, it's silly to get overburdened with high-tech apparati—but it's just as crazy to cling to horse-and-buggy P&E forever. Old assets with ROIs calculated on book values have outrageously high ROIs. If a manager of such an SBU is being rewarded in an incentive system that includes ROI, he or she won't want to update the operation when it should be.

AVOIDING HEAVY CAPITAL INTENSITY

Heavy capital intensity should be avoided like the plague. But that's easier said than done. Even with all the proper controls, you can still end up with a tremendous chunk of capital vis-á-vis your sales volume. What are the remedies for this?

One sure-fire cure for the investment-intense SBU is keeping capacity utilization up. Unfortunately, this pursuit can set off the management clutch response described in the last chapter. Care must be taken to ensure that your slack capacity is filled rationally. You don't want to find yourself explaining to management that in order to achieve full asset use you had to destroy the business.

Big market shares help mitigate the agonies of heavy capital intensity. By now you probably won't find that very surprising, since generous market shares seem to be capable of removing many of life's problems.

Another heavy investment cure is offering customers a broader line in a narrower market. The "sharp-focus-high-spectrum" strategy has the advantage of giving you a better learning curve over a wider range of items without getting far astray of your area of expertise.

Value strategies also help. For the high-investment SBU, a value strategy can raise you from a two-star to a four-star level of ROI. Of course, as with all the other strategies geared to get you out of the heavy capital intensity box, this one does so by raising sales volumes rationally. But that could be somewhat misleading. Since most of the remedies suggest that salvation can come from the marketing area, some readers might be sent hurtling off the deep end with the conclusion that the answer is simply to spend more on sales and marketing. Hold on! This is not a safe remedy. In fact, it could be suicidal. Look at the lower right box on the MagiCube. The ROI is so low there I've left it blank to dramatize the folly of this strategy.

The overriding consideration for any capital investment decision is whether it will help you better compete. That's the ultimate goal of any capital expenditure. Overspending leads to ruin. Underspending leaves you in a

MAGICUBE 8

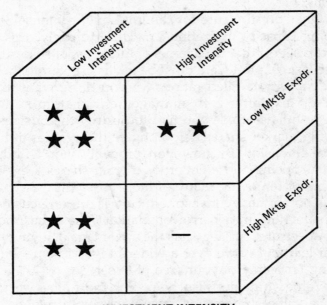

INVESTMENT INTENSITY
AND
MARKETING EXPENDITURES

weakened state. Somewhere in between lies the correct level of investment in any given business unit. You won't find the correct level without doing your homework. Nothing good ever comes out of a strategic analysis vacuum. You've got to think it all the way through.

Strateg-O-Gram:

CAPITAL INTENSITY CAN BE OFFSET BY LARGE MARKET SHARES, LINE BROADENING, AND VALUE STRATEGIES. AVOID EXCESSIVE SALES & MARKETING SPENDING.

chapter nineteen
Mergers and Acquisitions

"Smokestack Flange's gotta make some dramatic moves on
The Street. Like a big merger or a tricky LBO," declared
Bunkman.
"What you're saying is we should invest our Harvard
education in highwire acts that won't cure corporate
disease," challenged Link.
"The world expects more from our highly honed Harvard
intellects," chimed in Squint.

T. Haller, *Link Dover at Harvard Business School*

I suppose few of us are ever going to be players in a big
merger. It's fun to read about them though. Still, if you
own a small business you might have occasional opportunities to join forces with others in a similar or com-
plementary business. The commonplace lures are the efficiencies of a bigger scale, synergy, line broadening,
united-we-stand-divided-we-fall thinking, and so forth.
You wouldn't surmise it when you read about the major
mergers, but the merger decision should be basically a
strategic decision. The rules should be no different than

those already amply explained in this book. Unfortunately, in the real world mergers are not culminated as extensions of corporate strategy. Consequently, they seldom turn out well. Anywhere from a third to three-quarters turn out disappointing. The executives who perpetrate them should afterwards, following my son's most famous household malapropism, "slink away and lick their heels."

If the merged entity won't have the basic strategic strengths this book preaches, then why bother? One of the many unsavory examples in recent times was when Pan Am gobbled up National Airlines. The merger looked like a natural: a strong international line joining a burly U.S. line. It should have spelled market power, enhanced efficiency, and avid reciprocity. But it was not to be. The two lines had quite different strategic philosophies and work forces. Melding them turned out to be nigh to impossible. It looked great on paper—as many mergers do—but the deal turned out to be an enormous headache that many a perceptive strategist might have predicted.

It's no mystery why so many top executives catch merger fever. Mergers are just what any ego needs. Mergers can make you feel tough and powerful—like a cowboy ropin' 'n' brandin' steers. Some executives get to thinking anything they acquire—no matter how bad it is strategically—can be molded into a world-class money-printing machine with their bare hands.

Unfortunately, few folks really can brandish such power when the strategic rationale for the merger is absent. The deck is stacked against them. No contingent of high-priced investment bankers and legal minds can turn a poor strategic bet into a good one.

Most of these folks—as intelligent as they may be—wouldn't know a strategy if it bit them. But as Camus once said, "Man is a creature who spends his entire life in an attempt to convince himself he is not absurd." So they pile on layer after layer of legal arguments that detract participants in the merger from the real point of the whole deal: to strengthen business strategies.

For the simple one-SBU business, the strategic rationale necessary for successful mergers can be discovered in the preceding chapters. For complex multi-SBU businesses, however, there are some additional tips found in Chapter 21.

Strateg-O-Gram:

ACQUISITIONS MUST FOLLOW STRATEGIC LAWS.

chapter twenty
Incentives

Fear is a powerful force. A management weapon. Fear gets
results and it's easy to dish out. But fear also has miserable
side-effects: low morale, ass-covering, back-biting, high
turnover, to name a few.

There are better methods for getting results, such as
cash incentives. Many companies have elaborate incentive
programs based on worker's performance. Unfortunately,
most incentive programs reward workers for the wrong
reasons. They're too tactical to be much good as motivat-
ing tools. Yet, with little extra effort, the run-of-the-mill
incentive program can be converted into a powerful
strategic tool. Certain strategic factors, which have been
mentioned, are important for any given business unit.

These are the components upon which to build the successful incentive program.

People should be rewarded for successfully implementing the business firm's official strategies, not for chasing after objectives that make little or no difference in the final results. As my malaprop son would say, "That's a self-defeating circle."

For example, why reward the manager who achieves a big initial sales volume on a new product that has such poor quality it'll never earn any repeat sales? That's sheer madness. The reward should be geared to the product's relative quality and to its long-term market share attainment.

There is an added plus from having a strategy-based incentive program. It makes sure your workers know what your strategy is.

Don't ever make the mistake of assuming your workers automatically know what strategy your business is founded on. I've seen too many employee surveys to indicate otherwise. You can hold seminars for employees, post bulletins, send a monthly newsletter, and still they won't alter their work habits until they see, in dollars and cents, how it all applies to their pocketbook.

Incentive programs based on strategic factors are robust communication vehicles. In fact, I'd say they were mandatory if you really want to see your strategies executed.

Strateg-O-Gram:

INCENTIVE PROGRAMS MUST BE BASED ON STRATEGIC FACTORS.

chapter twenty-one
The Corporate Matrix

Then Dr. Success rose to speak. His voice was strong and
he was sort of chanting when he began:
"I say unto thee that there are no corporate strategies.
Verily, thine leaders have misled thee. They have
beclouded thine eyes to the matrix."

T. Haller, *Dr. Success*

Strategies are formulated and carried out at the SBU-level
not at the corporate level. Of course, hardly anyone pays
any attention to this fact. This is one more reason why
many American industries dither like retired English
brigadiers. Still, if you have more than one business unit,
it gets very confusing keeping them all straight. Fortunately, strategists have invented a few simple ways of
helping you.

The most common help is the famous Market Matrix
of the Boston Consulting Group. It looks like this (and I'm
sure you've seen it before):

84

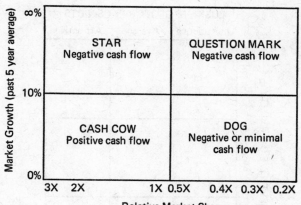

MARKET MATRIX

As you can readily see, a lot of what we said about market share and growth markets comes to life in this simple matrix. (Note where you produce the positive cash flow.) This is an easy matrix to draw up. Just make sure you've got your SBUs defined. The common mistake is to study whole families of products (like the entire automotive market) in one sweep and then wonder why the matrix doesn't make any sense. Plot all your own SBUs, along with the competitive ones, to bring this visual to life.

Another popular matrix is the Directional Policy Matrix. The DPM is more thorough than the Market Matrix because it encompasses more than merely the market share and market growth rate. It's also geared to show your potential, rather than your current posture. It looks like this:

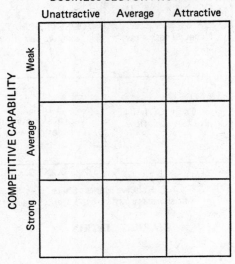

BUSINESS SECTOR PROSPECTS

DIRECTIONAL POLICY MATRIX

The Business Sector Prospects pulls together these factors: market growth rate, profit stability, margin maintenance ease, product differentiation ease, number of competitors, and the clout of the biggies. It also evaluates the allure of the market (is everyone and his brother slavering to get into it?), the danger of impending substitutes, the danger of raw material shortages, and stuff like that. In other words, what factors make this market sexy or a turn-off?

Competitive Capability is where you fit in. It covers your share (or it's honestly forecasted level in the near term), your manufacturing capability, your R&D talent, and so on. Objectivity is important here. It won't work otherwise, so don't play games.

Plot both your SBUs and competition's. It's pretty obvious where you'd want most of yours to end up on this matrix. The normal corporation won't have all winners, but it should have some if it expects to be around in the future. And if you have too many weaklings you have two choices: fish or cut bait. Review each weakling SBU to see if there's anywhere you can bolster its strategies. If the situation looks hopeless—or it'd be too costly to restrategize—the only solution is to milk the SBU (i.e., manage it for cash) until it's dry, then sell it off.

There are many other matrices. One that I favor (not only because I invented it) is the Basic Success Ambience Matrix* because it includes the consumer in its scheme.

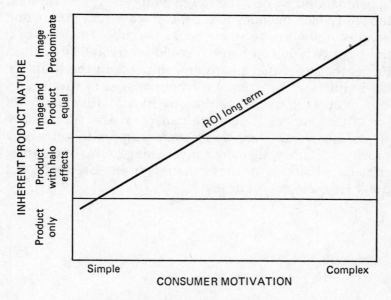

BASIC SUCCESS AMBIENCE MATRIX

The magnificence of the BSA Matrix is in this erudite concept: The more sophisticated your product (or service) and the more elaborate the consumer's perceived needs, the more dough you can make if you play your cards right. I don't mind saying that the BSA Matrix is clearly the most beautiful management tool available today.

You can make the BSA Matrix even more powerful by adding a second version to the one pictured here. This would have the same vertical data but the horizontal would carry something I call "Industry Personality." This data deals with the relative sophistication of the market's competitors, how easy it is to get oneself established in this market, its competitive styles, its market share relationships, and so on. The range would be from crude on the left (which means you'd have an easy time competing because nobody who reads books is crude) to elegant on the right (where competition could be tricky). Implicit in this is the belief that the more competition, the healthier the industry is for everyone who manages to survive.

In all seriousness, neither my BSA Matrix nor any of the other matrices shown are panaceas. They don't have all the answers. They don't even purport to solve any problems. Rather, they are convenient pictures of complex strategic situations for multibusiness firms. Use them, but don't let them run your life.

chapter twenty-two
Stock Prices

That afternoon Dr. Success appeared again. He sported a
gold lamé business suit with a *Wall Street Journal* tucked
under the arm. Helped onto his marble podium, he paused
and looked at his audience. He knew how to work a crowd.
Thirty thousand people, but his eyes found me. He began:
"For there is a proximate cause and a prime cause. And the
price of stock is governed by both. But I say unto thee, it is
the prime cause that is the greater. Behold, the
Ultimate—the supreme force of the universe. Verily, the
Ultimate is strategy. For thine company is its strategy."

T. Haller, *Dr. Success*

The world catches on slowly. In 1543, Copernicus said the
earth zipped around the sun, but a hundred years later
Galileo was jailed for repeating it. Another hundred years
after that the Paris Observatory was still basing its work on
the old Ptolemaic theory. Even Sherlock Holmes believed
in an earth-centered cosmos. When Dr. Watson told him
the Ptolemaic theory had a competitor, Holmes said he
could not imagine the question was of any practical importance.

Intense patience is often required while we wait for the rest of the world to catch on to what we know to be true. Ask Wall Street mavens this question and watch them squirm: "What causes profit?" Ask strategists the same question and they'll immediately tell you strategy is the cause of profit. If they read this book, they'd cite you chapter and verse.

Ask investors what causes stock prices to go up and down and they'll mumble a few carefully selected words about dividends, growth postures, mergers on the horizon, and so forth. Ask strategists, and they'll tell you the only thing that really counts is strategy.

It can get confusing for the lesser mortals. But it's not hard to straighten them out. Stock prices are caused by a balance between investors hopes and fears. Many investors look at past and future profits searching to find hope or to mitigate their fears. A modest few (too few in my way of thinking) also look at cash flow. What investors usually don't realize is that it's the company's business strategies that are behind both profit and cash flow. Some of the more savvy security analysts do realize this. They demand to know about a company's strategies before they recommend a buy. In the next few years, you're going to hear a lot more about this.

Meanwhile, for your own company, you should remember that its strategies have a mighty impact on its stock prices. If you are in charge of financial relations, you may want to keep this in mind when speaking to the investment community.

If you are investing in the stock market,, you may want to study the strategies of your investment candidates. When you're not an insider it's hard to get a grip on a company's business strategies without resorting to a lot of independent research and some reading between the lines. A few companies give a pretty good rundown on their strategies in their annual statements. Others cover them in separate news releases to the financial community that frequently get coverage in the business press. (Since reading this book puts you well on the road to becoming a master strategist, you wouldn't have to necessarily accept everything they tell you in these missives.) More companies are starting to sense the prudence of telling about their strategies. And others will do this as the years roll by.

Those that tell the best strategy story are going to be the ones that investors become most interested in. After all, when you come right down to it, that's what people invest in—a company's strategies. It's all very simple really.

Strateg-O-Gram:

STRATEGY GOVERNS STOCK PRICES.

chapter twenty-three
Compulsory Chapter on Japanese Management Modes

He loaded the cassette and flicked on the machine.
"It's a tape of a Japanese quality circle. The leader reads
passages from the latest American bestseller on super-fast
management techniques," my guide explained.
I didn't understand the language of course, but the camera
kept panning to the quality circle members who were all
laughing. Then there was some Japanese writing on the
screen and the tape ended. I asked what the writing said.
"It said: 'WITH AMERICA AS OUR COMPETITOR,
JAPAN CAN'T LOSE,'" my guide told me.

T. Haller, *Dr. Success*

(Note: A chapter describing Japanese management methods is required, by United Nations Protocol No. 79-06UN, in all business books published in the world.)

Did I hear someone ask if we should follow the procedures of the land of the rising sun? Well, I'm surprised people are still asking that question. But let's get it over with before we get into the second section of this book and the Big Power Trip.

You must be pretty tired of hearing about how marvelous the Japanese are. High quality products. Willing, grinning, bowing workers. Consensus. Ad nauseum. Actually, it's not true and some Americans are starting to catch on. But we still have quite a large pack of self-styled experts making the corporate rounds who want us all to emulate glorious Nippon.

We're not like the Japanese, never will be, and shouldn't want to be. The Japanese are doing what they do because they have no other choice. They live on a dumpy island with bad roads and virtually no natural resources. They have no future unless they continue to work their tails off. That includes crash courses to prepare kids for entrance exams to get into kindergarten. The school days start early and end late. The kids suffer from stress and fatigue. Japanese life is one long struggle filled with fierce competition, boring meetings, compromised unions, and serf-like obedience to managerial overlords.

Surveys show that Japanese workers are less happy than Americans, less proud of their work, and even less willing to fight for their country. Not exactly the two-fisted kind of country where I'd want to live.

Japan is a land with hardly any ethnic diversity. IQ tests suggest they are smarter than we are. We average 100, the Japanese 111 on the standard IQ testing methods. If these tests are indicative (and what do I know?), it gives them certain advantages in the industrial area that we could not hope to match, so let's stop worrying about it—and let's just get on with the job the best way we know how. We can manage our way out of this disparity if it is a problem. On the other hand, there's no evidence that says, collectively, we need an extra 11 IQ points to compete in the world. Who said success just took brains?

We need to stop trying to copy Japanese industrialists and devise our own native-born solutions. One place to start is with our strategic options. The Japanese are not that sophisticated strategically, just lucky. We can run circles around them if we grow up strategically and intellectually. This means using our brains a bit more earnestly. More hard strategic thinking is what it comes down to. In the long run strategy governs our destiny—not ethnic culture.

Thus ends the first part of this book. You are now a strategist. We now move on to Part II in which we outline the steps and methods necessary to use this knowledge about strategy to acquire corporate power.

II

THE POWER

Power, money, and intellectual challenge are what most of us get from our jobs. Of the three, power is the most satisfying. Few people acquire corporate power who are not also master strategists. But that alone is not enough. There are methods that strategists must use to acquire power, and these are explained in the next few chapters.

chapter twenty-four
Power: How Not to Get It

"When I'm boss people'll jump or get the sack," boasted
Bunkie.
"Or be so scared they'll find ways to avoid you," Link
cautioned.

T. Haller, *Link Dover at Harvard Business School*

Having become the complete strategist, you can now acquire power. But not just any kind of power. You should go for the right kind of power. Some kinds of power are less effective than others. The kind to stay away from is the power that induces fear. In Chapter 20, I commented on how fear was not the optimum incentive. Still, the prevalent impression is that power-produced fear is close to being universal. A survey indicated that 70% of us think we are being motivated by fear.[1]

Of course, this fact doesn't mean all fear is negative. Some fear can be positive. Fearing that you may not be

[1]David Grant, "The Ultimate Power," the Steve King Show, WIND-Radio, April 26, 1983.

able to afford a winter fling in Colorado makes you work harder to earn enough money. Fear of Soviet attack has a lot to do with wanting to keep our national defenses strong. Fear isn't all bad. And sometimes we don't really know what's good for us. Nonetheless, fear is a very unsafe management tool. For strategists, it is a tool that is most unlikely to produce positive results. Fear is, however, sufficiently widespread that many readers may assume it to be the easiest and fastest road to power. It isn't, and the following story illustrates this point.

An old friend had a boss whose clumsy methods made people literally grovel in fear. One time he proclaimed nobody in his department could schedule a vacation during a certain month. Immediately, a black pall descended over his department. Rumors flew. There'd be a major reorganization that month. Many would be fired or demoted. Production fell off. Finally, my friend summoned forth the courage to ask his boss what was so special about that month. "I'm taking some vacation then," his boss said, "And I just figured we should try to keep the key people in the office while I'm away." That was all there was to it. But this simple episode had caused a lot of needless squirming and lowered production. The boss's problem was a heavy-handed, mindless quest for corporate power that made him almost flamboyantly devious. Like many of his type who develop such errant instincts, his every utterance was routinely misinterpreted. Each gruff remark fed the general terror in his department. This was certainly not his intent, but the signals in his department were so mixed he eventually had to be replaced. He had wanted power more than most. But he went after it in the wrong way and lost.

Among those who prefer power to sex the need is so obsessive that almost anything that frustrates their pursuit of power throws them off balance. What would be just a normal roadblock to others can almost drive them daffy.

I knew of another boss whose lust for power was so visceral that veins in his forehead engorged and formed a raised "V" everytime he attended a meeting. The conference room was his battlefield, but power always eluded him. The truth was this boss was a lightweight playing in a heavyweight's league. Near the end it was pitiful to watch h**i**m. He just didn't know how to go about it. His former lieutenants remember, with John Deanlike total recall, one looney staff meeting where they were trying to brief him for a big meeting in which the fate of some new brand would be decided. One guy was chosen to brief him and the others sat there and watched. The veins in the boss's forehead throbbed as he began.

BOSS:	Tell me everything I need to know before I go into that meeting.
PRODUCT MANAGER:	Well, after three months in the market the brand's market share is below estimate at only 8.3%.
BOSS:	Do I really need to know that?
PRODUCT MANAGER:	(Faltering.) Ummm, let's see. Well, distribution is effectively complete. The brand got a 92% on an all-commodity basis, which isn't bad.
BOSS:	Do I really need to know that?
PRODUCT MANAGER:	(Getting nervous.) Well, our attitude study shows that the brand has a pretty bad negative. Specifically, consumers think it's too. . . .
BOSS:	(Cutting him off.) Do I need to know that for this meeting?

This sequence was repeated five or six more times until the product manager had run out of things to say. Finally, the boss said:

BOSS:	Dammit! You haven't told me a damn thing. What you're saying is I don't need to know anything in order to go to that meeting!

Not long after this boss was transferred to a position

where he could work alone. Real corporate power was never to be his. According to those that still remember him, he was the inveterate tactician: a rather sad example of the manager who never matures beyond entry-level skills. They never go very far because they think the combination of fear and tactical moxy can lead to the executive suite.

Those who choose to play up their strategic strengths should take pains to differentiate effective power from ostensible power. Not everybody who acquires power is operating with a full deck, even when they eschew fear.

Take Gandhi for example. Maybe he wasn't the first sexual whacko to receive immense power, but his power was not guided by an effective and balanced political strategy. Gandhi seemed preoccupied by far-out nonstrategic concerns. He generously dispensed dietary advice to the poor Hindu hordes without himself ever having heard of protein or vitamins. One time he lurked near death and his doctors found he had been on diet of only ground nut-butter and lemon juice. When his pneumoniac wife was fading he refused to let her have penicillin, arguing that alien substances should not be introduced into the body. Accordingly, his wife died. Shortly afterward Gandhi contracted malaria and accepted shots of quinine. Here was a man who wielded immense power over hundreds of millions of people, yet were his strategies effective? What remains today of his legacy besides a distorted Oscar-winning movie?

There's power and then there's power. Choose wisely. If your career is to be as rewarding as you want it to be, and if this country is to experience its industrial renaissance, the strategist is the one who must wield the batons of power. Even on a less philosophic level, power is essential. In the corporate arena it's absolutely critical that you gain power in order to protect your own skin. You won't go far if your fate is controlled by others.

To be effective here you have to find a way that eliminates power's negative effects. Fear and irrational managerial modes are not the most universally productive ways of running the enterprise. Things are bad enough already in most firms. An American Management Association poll of 1500 middle managers found that 67% did not trust the top officers of their companies.[2] The strategist who can help change that insidious climate will go places. For one thing, in such a climate, he or she will be granted ready support from the troops longing to place their trust in someone who is guided by a sounder and more predictable rationale.

The question is: What is the right way to acquire and use power?

[2]"Middle Managers Suffer from Low Morale, a New Study Suggests," *Wall Street Journal*, January 3, 1984, p. 1.

chapter twenty-five
What Should the Strategist Know About Power?

"I'll join the right club and hobnob with corporate biggies,"
Bunkie told his study group while discussing career
futures.
"But becoming indispensable requires a sterling
character . . ." began Squint.
". . . And the steel-trap mind of a strategist," added Link.

T. Haller, *Link Dover at Harvard Business School*

Organizational power has a lot to do with dependence. If you're dependent on someone, you're in that person's power. The person who dictates how much you get paid has power over you. So does the person who feeds you information you can't do without. Get the picture?

Within any organization you can acquire power by monopolizing and wielding information the organization can't live without. Of course, not any kind of information will do. It has to be central to the corporation's basic needs.[1]

Absolute power is not easy to acquire if you are on

[1]Richard H. Emerson, "Power-Dependence Relationships," *American Sociological Review*, Vol. 27 (1962), pp. 31–41.

the lower rungs of a big organization. But it's never too soon to start. You're going to get power by formulating business strategies, but first you must apply some simple logic.

Organizational power is related to the following factors: (1) your access to people and information, (2) your length of time in the organization because it increases your access to people and to information, (3) extent to which you acquire expert knowledge not possessed by higher ranking managers.

These factors make you difficult to replace. So if you make these factors work in your favor, you automatically continue to acquire more power. The more expert you become, the harder it is for the company to dump you. Finally, the more upper management grows to depend on your expertise, the more your power becomes increasingly relevant to the company.[2]

Unquestionably, the single area of expertise most admired and needed by the corporation is strategy formulation. No one can argue with that. The officers of any company will gladly overlook your managerial faults if you persist in coming up with strategies that make them look good to stockholders. When you become your company's leading authority on strategy you make yourself virtually irreplaceable. Strategy is your obvious ticket to the corridors of corporate power.

Strategic power is clean power. It's not the dirty kind usually associated with office politics. It's clean because it accommodates the corporation to the realities it faces internally and externally. The dirty kind of politics—reliant on grasping for control and disinformation—buffers the company from this reality. Dirty politics drags the organization away from its goals. The pure power of strategy

[2]David Mechanic, "Sources of Power of Lower Participants in Complex Organizations," *Administrative Quarterly*, Vol. 7, No. 3 (Dec. 1962), pp. 349–64.

keeps the company locked on its true trajectory. I don't mean to preach ethics to you. Your own conscience is your guide. My point is a pragmatic one. The pure power that derives from strategic skills is more useful to the company; hence, to a large extent, it serves as a buffer protecting your career from the machinations of the merchants of dirty power.

An American Management Association article entitled "Who Gets Power—and How They Hold on to It: A Strategic-Contingency Model of Power" says that the people "most able to cope with the organization's critical problems and uncertainties acquire power."[3] For example, your legal department might acquire inordinate power for a spell while the firm's existence is threatened by hefty liability suits. Once the danger is removed, the legal department reverts to its more normal power mode.

The element of strategy is always critical. External uncertainty and internal opportunities are constantly arising. There is no point in any company's history where strategic decisions do not need to be forged. Strategic decision-making is central to, and a permanent concern of, all corporations. The AMA article adds that "power organizes around scarce and critical resources (and) rarely . . . around abundant resources."[4] Strategic skills will always be in great demand. There will always be a plethora of tacticians and a shortage of strategists. Only sound strategic thinking can alleviate the firm of its gnawing uncertainties.

Giving your company the gift of certitude is an act of power—it's almost paternal—that results in the acquisition of yet more power. It becomes self-perpetuating.

[3]Gerald Salancik and Jeffrey Pfeffer, "Who Gets Power—and How They Hold on to It: A Strategic-Contingency Model of Power," *Organizational Dynamics*, Winter 1977, copyright 1977 by AMACON, a division of the American Management Association, Inc., pp. 98–100.

[4]Salancik and Pfeffer, p. 101.

chapter twenty-six
Arranging to Get Power

"Quick," said Link, "Name any powerful industrial or
political figure who is not a master strategist."
Silence reigned.

T. Haller, *Link Dover at Harvard Business School*

Strategy will be the vehicle that lifts you into the ranks of
the powerful. How do you get the ball rolling? First, you
develop a special set of radar antennae that lets you pick
up political undercurrents. All strategies are, or become,
woven into the company's political fabric. You could say
strategies have "face" riding on them.

You don't want to appear to be a champion of overtly,
aggressively, radical strategies. Instead, when change is
necessary, ease toward it gradually. This way you won't
create enemies—well, not any more than necessary.

Train your antennae to detect what is really wanted
and needed. Cautious people won't always level with you.
The values they espouse may be quite different from those
they really subscribe to. They may be keeping their true
intentions half-hidden. (That's one of the rules of old-

fashioned dirty politics.) Consequently, it is important to understand and appreciate the corporate culture. Even the best strategies won't click if the corporate culture is incapable of delivering. There may simply be too low an intellectual level to fathom all the strategic ramifications you are talking about. Or there may be tremendous resistance to change. Or, as with many successful companies, they may feel no improvements are possible. None of these situations is that uncommon. I once had a close-up view of a corporate culture possessing all of those neuroses.

I had just been transferred to a different department and was asked by the manager to draw up a five-year plan. After thinking about it, and working very hard on it, I finally submitted it to him. After a couple of weeks I asked the manager if my plan was okay and if we should start implementing it. He said he hadn't read it, but would get back to me. Several follow-ups over the next three months still produced no response. I finally stopped asking. Five years later, when my boss was on vacation, I was in his office tracking down some stray report. I spotted a shipping carton—the kind movers use—under his desk and asked his secretary if the missing report might be inside. "Oh, that box," she laughed, "No, it wouldn't be—that box's been sitting there, still sealed, since we moved to our new offices four years ago." The box was marked "Current Projects," but had been unopened since our move. What the hell, I thought, the tape is dried out; he'll never notice. I opened it and found my five-year plan in a file marked "Urgent." Of course, by this time it didn't really matter. My plan had long since been executed so subtly no one noticed I had no authority to do so.

For some people, the agony of decision-making prompts procrastination. Five years is a bit extreme, but the corporate culture simply did not reinforce or reward strategic pursuits. This then means you are free to do it on your own.

You should not be dumbfounded to find yourself surrounded by a circle of hopelessly tactical wheel-spinners. Such a lame-brain milieu is hog-heaven to the strategist. Fortunately, such companies are easy to find. And a power grab in that type of company is child's play.

The strategy-minded company is also a healthy place to strut your stuff. But here it's not played out in elementary moves.

But each environment requires a different approach largely based on the kind of language you use. The first situation requires easy concepts and small initial steps. The second one calls for a loftier approach. But in both the laws of strategy are the same.

chapter twenty-seven
Implementing Your Power Plan With Examples

"True intellectuals don't need examples. The theory is
enough," sniffed Bunkie.
"Screw the intellectual. I wanna be a businessman. Give
me an example," said Squint.

T. Haller, *Link Dover at Harvard Business School*

Few people are going to take the trouble to study a book
about strategy. Having done it, you have the advantage
over them. Your competition won't be very stiff. (Even if
they do read this book, they will soon forget it as they
lurch on to yet another book seeking simple solutions to
their stalemated careers.) To put strategy to use in the real
world, you'll have to make it look like you didn't get it out
of some book. That'd kill it faster than saying you heard
about it on "The Phil Donahue Show."

Weave your strategy into a selection of anecdotes,
which is what Americans like best. Laws and principles
put people to sleep. That's why your local TV news covers
fires. The principle that fires destroy and kill is appar-
ently not sufficient; the example must be reiterated each

night. It's stupid, but you aren't going to change it. It is a nation of examples.

I know a guy who, 20 years ago, worked on the introduction of a margarine brand. Going by his stories, which I've always doubted by the way, he learned every lesson of strategy from this one spare experience. If you've been paying close attention to this book you know a single paltry SBU can't teach you a great deal about strategy. Nonetheless, margarine buttered this guy's career path for two decades because, instead of lecturing, he had interesting stories to tell. (That's why Americans like examples—it's not like being back in school.) You are going to be pitted against people like my margarine czar, so you'll need your own portfolio of juicy examples.

If you're at a junior level, it's kind of risky to use examples from your own company. Veteran corporate burnouts can be conveniently flexible on company history. They'll be able to bring up counterarguments too easily, regardless of the facts. It's a game you can't win.

Your examples, therefore, should come from other companies, preferably other industries. If you're young, you'd be advised to keep them fairly current. It's one time when not having gray hair can be a drawback.

The business press is full of such illustrations. Clip and file them away. The best ones will be those that are reflective and analytical rather than just simple news items. Someone's always going to ask you for an example. You'd better be prepared. Otherwise, you'll sound too much like a scholar and not enough like a hands-on manager.

One more thing: You never heard of me, or this book. Get it?

chapter twenty-eight
Is Strategy A Team Task?

"From now on I wanna be captain of this study team,"
announced Bunkie.
"But then it would no longer be a team," Link replied with
impeccable logic.

T. Haller, *Link Dover at Harvard Business School*

A team differs from the normal group organization. Team members share power equally. Not so hot an idea when you want the power to yourself. Some teams have captains, but he or she doesn't get to have extra power as a rule, just the added burden of being a coordinator.

Teams are popular in management literature. They reflect our innate sense of democracy, maybe. We've been led to believe that teams were instrumental in Japan's industrial success story.

Is the formulation of strategy a logical task for teamwork? Or should strategies be developed by the old boss-subordinate system?

My choice would be to avoid teams. Strategy is too important. Teams are okay for assembling and assessing tactical plans. Your company won't crash if some tactical effort comes a cropper. But crummy strategies will bring forth total ruin. If your team makes a mistake in its formulation of strategy, you'll get tarred with the same brush and may lose your power base.

I'm sorry, sportsfans, if this sounds like heresy. But I've got some sound reasons for not wanting to trust any team to such a critical task—apart from the obvious evidence that, even in the sports world, team effort is largely a myth: the star system makes mincemeat of it.

The business organization actually gives a better environment for team play than does the athletic field. But, for an entirely different set of reasons, team work frequently produces worse business decisions (and strategies) than old-fashioned despotism.

With the best and the brightest—people like Robert McNamara, Dean Rusk, Bobby Kennedy, McGeorge Bundy and Arthur Schlesinger, Jr.—planning the Bay of Pigs invasion, how could it have gone so wrong? Or as JFK asked: "How could we have been so stupid?"

The reason is embodied in Janis' Law:

> The more . . . esprit de corps there is [in] a policy-making ingroup, the greater the danger that independent critical thinking will be replaced by groupthink, which is likely to result in irrational . . . actions. . . ."[1]

Teams develop counterproductive habits. Probably because of something called "group cohesiveness and reinforcement," teams start thinking they're invulnerable. This makes them overoptimistic and willing to take bigger risks than they should.

The U.S. Navy illustrated this point just before Pearl Harbor. As you may recall, naval intelligence lost contact

[1] Irving L. Janis, "Groupthink," *Psychology Today*, November 1971, p. 32.

with the Japanese armada on December 6th, 1941. Any-body get upset about this? No, it wasn't thought to be a big deal—the U.S. Navy was invulnerable. Admiral Kim-mel actually joked about: "Do you mean they could be rounding Diamond Head and you wouldn't know it?" There was no panic. The soporific weekend at Pearl Harbor continued as normal until early Sunday morning, De-cember 7th.

The team also applies pressure against any member who voices dissent. The Bay-of-Pigs planning team had only one member with any serious reservations: Arthur Schlesinger, Jr. JFK didn't let him join in the final vote. The team had successfully ousted him.

During the heavy bombing of North Vietnam, Lyn-don Johnson found a dissenter on his team: Bill Moyers. He used to mockingly call Moyers "Mr. Stop-the-Bombing." Teams share the illusion of unanimity; and they will silence their dissenting members in order to pro-duce this illusion.

The illusion of unanimity leads to another feeling: that the team must be right. "If we're all the best the country has to offer, and if we all agree, then our decisions must be infallible." Going by their memoirs, most of the Bay-of-Pigs team members had reservations about the Cuban invasion plan all along. But, besides Schlesinger, no one spoke up. Consensus was assumed, but later they would all read in each other's memoirs that everyone had different assumptions about the invasion plan.

These blemishes on the team concept mean that there is seldom a complete airing of the issues. This makes strategic formulation very difficult. As you can see from the chapter headings in this book, there are many issues that must be weighed and discussed before you will feel confident about the validity of your plan. Teams don't give you the freedom of speech you need to do this properly.

Teams also seldom like to go outside the group. They are distrustful of nonmembers. They don't like to bring in outside experts for advice or information. They want to do it all themselves because of feelings of invulnerability and unanimity. Moreover, if any expert does happen to break through to them, the team will leap on any argument that supports its own and reject any that opposes it.

Finally, and this is the reason that makes teams the most unlikely source of strategic wisdom, the team will seldom draft any contingency plan. Teams simply don't want to grant that their ideas won't pan out. Teams never expect setbacks. Teams think they are, as I said, invulnerable, and always right. Teams can work at the tactical level, but not at the strategic.

For these reasons, your quest for power via strategy, should become an individual effort. You can't really share power anyway. You can delegate it—but that's different. Power is fleeting. Once you get it, don't risk losing it because you wanted to share it with some team.

chapter twenty-nine
Strategic Management

"How is our study group's working relationship disrupted
by our new case analysis strategy?" asked Link.
"Because I can no longer sit next to Mary," declared
Bunkie.

T. Haller, *Link Dover at Harvard Business School*

Businesses fail because they follow the wrong strategies.
That's axiomatic But why do they follow the wrong
strategies?

There are several reasons. The chief reason is that
they think past experience can be their guide. There are
red-alert problems with this notion. Strategy cannot be
derived from personal experience. That's because your
personal experience is too limited to cover all the factors
that make up strategy, under all the permutations possible. Furthermore, the circumstances under which you
lived those strategies will never be repeated again. Not
exactly anyway. But in too many companies it's still experience that rules the day. No matter how misguided this
is.

The use of past experience generally escapes analysis. Events are assumed to form connections as in primitive ritual religions. Business outcomes are sloppily thought to be caused by the things that preceded them. It's largely a post hoc kind of thinking. If you studied formal logic—you know this isn't valid. But here's how it goes: Someone runs a cents-off deal, for example, and sales go up and the company concludes that the cents-off deal propelled the sales increase. Thereafter, it becomes company lore that all brands must have cents-off deals. In parallel fashion, I know of cigarette companies that will spend millions every year handing out those little four-cigarette samples without once having done any testing to see if samples (on very old brands that most smokers have already tried many times) make sound business sense. It is almost impossible to shake folks out of their deeply entrenched "religious" beliefs.

In some companies, strategies fail because they are hammered out by parochials who don't actually understand how the rest of the corporation functions. Some noted fast-trackers have displayed this tunnel-vision problem. It has been said that one of the bases of John DeLorean's failure was that he had not appreciated how GM produced his early career success. Out on his own, without GM's impressive staff resources, DeLorean was the victim of his own—heretofore unnoticed—limitations.[1]

Strategies embrace all personnel and require their commitment to succeed. A new strategic plan can meet resistance all the way down the line when the troops are not involved in the strategy's formulation. Some organizations are more participative than others. That maudlin

---

[1]"What's Good for General Motors," *USA Today*, April 8, 1983, p. 3C, quoting from the April 1983 issue of *Inc.* magazine, a cover story by Craig R. Waters entitled "DeLorean."

social-worker word "sharing" has crept into their voc-
abularies. Resistance can be overcome by involving as
many SBU people in the strategy forging process as possible. A feeling of having participated will accelerate group
acceptance of a new strategic plan.

But it would be wrong to suppose that nonparticipa-
tion is the major source of resistance. The root cause of
resistance is usually something else altogether. It is a fear
of a change in working relationships, which isn't as frivolous as it sounds. Most work is routine and it's the human
relationships on the job that help make the work environment tolerable. Such relationships take years to build.
New marching orders that threaten to mess up these relationships are not going to be welcomed.

Successful strategic management calls for implementation plans that dismantle as few personal links as possible. When you announce a new strategy, you should take
pains to emphasize how these relationships will remain
the same. If it is absolutely essential to alter them, it
should be done as gently as possible—perhaps gradually,
rather than suddenly.

chapter thirty

Things Will Be Great for the Strategist

"We have our whole lives ahead of us," said Squint looking
off into the distance.
"Excellent observation," said Link.

T. Haller, *Link Dover at Harvard Business School*

At the risk of being branded an optimist, I'd say the future
is going to be great for this country. No one is going to
benefit from this more—or gain more power—than the
professional strategist. Any time the economy poises to
take off on an extended ascent the industrial drums start
pounding out the mixed signals. Plans get tossed together
in a hurry. Most of them rather badly. But this time it's
going to be different. We know a lot more about business
strategy now than we did the last time this nation went
upward bound. (That was right after World War II.)

This time people who understand strategy are going
to call the shots. There will be more individual successes
and fewer failures among qualified strategists, as the GNP
climbs for the next 25 years, than among any other group
of people.

117

Despite energy shocks and recessions this country has been creating new jobs like mad. We have been faster than Japan, and faster than Europe (which is actually losing jobs). And these jobs aren't all coming from the high tech sector either. High tech only accounts for 10% of new jobs created in the past decade and, in total, will account for a meager 6% of jobs by the year 2000.

Peter Drucker thinks our present economy resembles the U.S. and German economies of 1873—just before these two nations started a quarter century of incredible expansion. Drucker cites Schumpeter's theory on how entrepreneurial instincts made the U.S. and Germany so industrially vibrant during this era, and how the lack of the same instinct made England and France stagnate during that period.[1]

The entrepreneurial drive is once again alive in our land. As Drucker says, our newest companies "are organized for systematic entrepreneurship and purposeful innovation."[2] Today, it is the new, but small, company that supplies the bulk of new jobs. Nor are they all high tech or service industry jobs. A lot of them are found in fairly simple manufacturing concerns. And the one thing they all have in common is this: They all need sound strategies.

Well into the twenty-first century there will be a strong demand for people who know their business strategy. They are the people who will occupy the seats of corporate power. They will call the shots. They will get the recognition. They will receive the rewards.

---

[1]Peter Drucker, "Why America's Got so Many Jobs," *Wall Street Journal*, January 24, 1984, p. 28.
[2]Drucker, p. 28.

III

POWER PLAYS FOR WOMEN

"The world is dominated by power, and you'd better not be
weak, if you can help it."

Katharine Hepburn[1]

As this book demonstrates, strategy can be learned. But
only a fool would claim that's all there is to it. Naturally, it
should go without saying that once you've devised your
strategy you will have to convince a lot of other people of
its inherent value. And so, if you are a woman, the questions then become: Do women have the right stuff to pull
this off? And if they do have the right stuff, how should
they go about it?

[1]Barbara Lovenheim, "The Great Kate on Death, Life, Women and Men,"
Wall Street Journal, February 16, 1984, p. 26.

chapter thirty-one
Do Women Make Good Strategists?

"Bunkie, your strategy sucks. You left out the learning
curve, the segmentation activity, the added-value
approach, and the marketing concept trap. Now, here's my
strategy . . . ," Mary began.
"Oh shut up and show us your . . . ," blurted Bunkman,
growing very red in the face.

T. Haller, *Link Dover at Harvard Business School*

I read the papers and see all those stories about women
getting into business in droves. The press has a way of
making everything seem so novel. But only the magnitude
of female presence is new—at least in the consumer
marketing and advertising business I've known. My first
boss was a woman, and it seems over the years I've always
been working with or competing with female executives
on all organizational levels. So I'm going to let my experience guide me here.

First of all, there's always going to be prejudice
against women, just as there is prejudice against everyone
else. Men are just as snide about other men as they are

121

about women. Everyone is fair game. Gossip and backbiting is one way weaklings—regardless of sex—attempt to introduce a feeling of security into their jittery lives. It comes from fear, and, deep down, most folks are afraid.

I don't think there is anything you can do, or should do, about it. Management wants people who concentrate on getting the job done. Management will gladly withhold promotions from those preoccupied in searching for insults.

Political intrigue crops up in any group of three or more people. What women frequently regard as sexual harassment is often calculated political machination. Viewed that way it is more serious than sexual harassment per se and it requires a different solution.

A mistake some managerial women make is to combat politically inspired attacks with snide insults. This is not the most effective way to conduct the political infight. Men are usually better at this game. Notice how the successful male politician handles it. He seldom launches a direct counterattack. He will deflect an attack with humor, he will use delaying tactics, he will occasionally simply change the subject to something on a loftier plane.

A strategist must appear above the fray. Faint indications of emotional reaction and an absence of political toughness raise inevitable questions (no matter how unfair) of whether a woman can handle a strategic assignment. The fact that many women already have strategic accountabilities will not exonerate the individual woman who reveals traces of political vulnerability.

Becoming an effective strategist requires a leadership instinct. But that can be interpreted in different ways. Some think women seldom develop leadership talent. They still see the children in their own neighborhoods and observe little boys pushing and shoving to be top dogs while the little girls sit on the sidelines. They say this occurs even in those neighborhoods with a strong presence of successful feminist mothers. They conclude that leadership oozes from the glands. Some women even have told me that they are afraid anatomical differences bar them from ever achieving prominence in the strategic arena.

I believe all these assumptions are based on an incomplete definition of leadership. You don't really need elephantine traits. Your intellect will work just as well. Leadership has more than one possible form of manifestation.

My guess is that more women will take this book to heart than men. The publishing industry's statistics show that women do read more. It's my sincere belief that there's never going to be enough genuinely good strategic thinkers in the world. In this bleak environment anyone who can offer sensible insights on strategy, and who isn't deterred from this task by peripheral skirmishes, can be a hot commodity on the career market.

If a woman puts her intellect to work on learning strategy, while her male rivals rely on the old familiar standbys, her probability of success is magnified.

chapter thirty-two
Can the Network Help?

No feminist network can propel you to the top. Maybe it can help you get placed now and then, but thereafter you are on your own.

Mentors won't help much either. The guy who is willing to be a mentor probably doesn't have a firm understanding of internecine politics. Without that, how can he offer any useful advice?

It's the bottom-line result that counts. No company survives long without people who produce results. Even crack tacticians make little difference in the long run. Companies always need strategists. When the chips are down they don't care about the genitalia of their strategists. But first you have to convince them. I'm afraid if you surveyed the American public it'd tell you the best strategists would be men. That is a prejudicial reality women have to overcome.

Forget about legislation and legal challenges. The legal trade can get you in the door so you have a chance at traditional male jobs, and it can get you equal pay. But in the pantheon of business this is relatively petty stuff. We're talking strategy—the ultimate destiny of the corporate world. No lawyer is ever going to force an employer to fork over responsibility for formulating strategy. Even if the courts mandated a women into the V.P. of Strategy's office, no company would use your strategic plans if they didn't believe in them. It would be an awfully lonely job.

Women need to acquire a "strategic image." It must become part of their projected personna. But it shouldn't be too hard. The competition simply isn't that formidable. And whether rivals are male or female most folks in the business world—rather than studying the ins and outs of strategy—are reading very soft bestsellers on the latest panaceas in management lore. If, instead, you invest your time in understanding the science of strategy, you'll run circles around rivals struggling to find a place to apply their Rotarian platitudes. Deep down, your nonstrategist rival has the mind of George Babbitt.

Here's a question women have asked me. How can we get in on the strategy act if we're never invited onto the golf course where such things are decided? Or the lockerroom, or the club? You know what I mean. In the first place, not many strategies are nailed down out on the links. Those that are decided between holes aren't the right kind anyway. Strategies of the type we've been writing about can't be dreamed up on a golf course.

I realize the basis of these questions usually has a much deeper meaning. It implies that women have little access to the senior officers of the company, that they are kept in staff or divisional pigeon holes and, ergo, can't make a strong contribution to strategy formulation. I believe this latter viewpoint stems from an erroneous understanding of strategy. Strategy is SBU-oriented, not corporate. Most jobs are in SBUs, few are in corporate headquarters.

Okay, you say, but am I not just using clever words to make the problem go away? Isn't the fact that women are seldom on buddy-buddy terms with the corporate heavy breathers going to hurt their chances of becoming movers and shakers in the game of strategy? Probably not as much as you may think. It is common to over-rate the importance of this male bonding and buddy-buddy stuff. The buddies fire their buddies with dire frequency, so it cannot really count for much. I know a guy who was invited to his assistant's Long Island home for dinner, taken to a hockey game that evening, and then invited to sleep over for the night. The next morning they rode into work on the same train, talking and laughing like blood brothers. When they got to the office, the senior guy fired his host of the night before.

The supposed friendship you see between men is not as sincrere or as deep as you think. Alan Alda captured this in his movie "Four Seasons." There is a touching scene where Alda's friend, Jack Weston, is unbaring his soul, telling Alda about some deep-rooted and very troubling problem he is grappling with. Alda laughs at him for using clinical language. That's pretty much the extent of male friendsip, and that's why some men actually prefer female friends. But that's another story.

The basic reality is that everyone is interested principally in his or her own career. If someone or something can help advance that career it will be "embraced." It doesn't matter if it wears pants, a skirt, or if it's just an idea. If it works, it works.

It comes down to this: You've got to make your own opportunities. The need for strategists is critical and will always be a pressing concern in any company. Most business people don't have a very clear understanding of what it is all about. But you can learn it. You can establish yourself as a reliable source of strategic skills. It can become part of the self-package you are trying to sell. Your strategic personna. Your ticket to the corridors of power.

chapter thirty-three
Shaping the Strategic Personna

"I sincerely intend to have stature in the world of
commerce," declared Bunkie.
"Sheer physical bulk, eh," countered Mary Moneyham.

T. Haller, *Link Dover at Harvard Business School*

Modern science has noted that men have a physical bulk
greater than women. Bulk helps men seize control of
human events like meetings. They can attract attention to
themselves more easily than women with less bulk. By
corollary then, women seldom have a commanding presence. Some attract attention to themselves because they
are, by societally induced standards, nice to look at—but
that's not the same thing and, in fact, can be a disadvan-
tage in certain settings. The natural, logical conclusion
then is that women must be preceded by glowing reputa-
tions before they can overcome the disinterest men con-
quer by sheer physical stature and power. A woman can
triumph over her unintended and frequently unhelpful
anatomical signals by building a reputation as a strategic
thinker.

Begin by studying this book with the same intensity you'd prepare for a final exam. Then search for openings to use what you've learned. Introduce strategic points in meetings and in reports. Campaign to impress on anyone who can remotely affect your career that you are a strategist. It may take less effort than you suspect.

People selection is less scientific than it should be. Most managers have a difficult time deciding whom to promote. They find it virtually impossible to balance all those plusses and minuses. Often some simple factor outweighs all else. So, if you worked diligently to associate yourself with solid strategic thinking, this can become that outweighing factor in your favor. I've been in on enough discussions where managers tried to justify recommendations on whom they wanted to promote. I can hear the conversation now:

"But are you sure you want to promote her? There are lots of guys that could do the job."

"Yeah, I know. But the thing is she's probably the best strategist we have."

"Oh well, that's different. Good choice."

That may seem pretty shallow to you, but people selection is mainly hunch. When you mention "strategist" you're talking apple pie. I know it's superficial, but doesn't superficiality underlie many of life's major decisions? America votes on its presidents based on nonverbal impressions garnered from 30-second TV spots. We get married after courtships in which true character seldom emerges.

The corporate world strives to be more careful about its personnel decisions, but human nature intrudes. There are few Spocks on this planet. Women must learn to play the game. Since the odds are against women, they have to manipulate the hunch process.

Think of shaping your strategic personna as creating

an elegantly calculated advertising campaign. Advertising is rated in terms of its reach and its frequency. *Reach* in your campaign refers to the people you work under, those in other departments who may be able to reinforce your message through rumor or gossip, and anyone you want to impress with your strategic skills. Keep in mind that no one is married to a set job position. The porter may be a division president five years from now. Don't neglect a "media target" because he or she cannot currently do much for you.

Frequency refers to the number of impressions you would leave with each key person. Try to deliver two or three strategic messages a month in total. Be prepared to modify your campaign as it unfolds. The individuals you are targetting should be observed to see if they really understand what you are saying, if they are paying close attention, and if they seem capable of assessing the importance of strategy. You may have to do more missionary work here than you suspect. And your campaign may require frequent adjustments as it progresses.

chapter thirty-four
Why Your Personna Is Important

"What makes you think you're always so right?"
demanded Bunkie.
"Well, I did read the case, and I read the text—neither of
which you appear to have done," answered Mary
Moneyham.

T. Haller, *Link Dover at Harvard Business School*

The deck is stacked against most of us regardless of gender. The annointed ones, the jokers that get all the laurels and promotions, frequently possess determining characteristics that—in a rational world—shouldn't have anything to do with it.

But it's not a rational world. Just watch the local TV news shows. Christine Craft, the Kansas City anchor, gets canned because she wasn't good looking enough. Most TV news folks *are* good looking. This means you get the news read to you by Cromagnons with zero analytical ability. Few of them understand percentages. They confuse millions and billions. Numbers have no meaning to them. I once sat in astonishment as one Chicago newsguy, standing in the midst of a driving snowstorm, looked straight into the minicam and reported that the Streets Department had 135,000 snowplows out that night. The anchorperson accepted his figures without question. No one could see that it was preposterous.

Okay, now I'm finally getting to my point: The business world isn't all that much different. People happen to get promoted for very frivolous reasons. Ergo, they aren't necessarily good at what they do. They may look the part. But, like actors, they are sometimes just reading their lines. When presented with new concepts they are at a loss to know how to react. Moreover, since they've gotten this far on charm, they are complacent. They probably don't feel much of a need to do any homework.

But the hungry woman can do her homework. She can learn all about strategy. Then she can begin to establish her strategic image. She can receive encouragement from the knowledge that most of her competitors are not going to be doing the same thing.

Of course, men who are trapped in meaningless tactical roles should do the same thing. For the good of the nation, it doesn't matter whether men or women do it, as long as our industries get decent strategies. But few men are going to bother.

My suspicion is that more women will end up calling the strategic shots than men. I say that because my judgment tells me women will make a stronger effort. They will study harder. They will tackle intellectual things more strenuously than men because that's the best way they can compete. Consequently, more thoroughly than men, they will embrace the strategic concepts I'm writing about in this book.

Part III was both a warning to men and a note of

encouragement to women. It is also a bugle call to all tacticians. Your competition on the success ladder isn't that formidable. Take heart. The battle will be long and hard, but the fruits of victory will be worth it.

INDEX

A

Acquisitions, 79–81, 90
Advertising, 33, 45
Advertising agencies, 11, 17,
    19
Automation, 65–73

B

Basic Success Ambience
    Matrix, 85–87
Bay of Pigs, 111–112
Boston Consulting Group,
    84–85
Breadth of line, 55, 77, 79
Business strategy, 6

C

Capacity, 45, 77
Cash flow, 44, 47, 48–51, 75,
    85, 90
Commodity, 32
Corporate matrix, 84–88

D

Delegating, 113
De Lorean, 115
Differentiation, 26–29, 33
Directional Policy Matrix,
    85–87
Discounters, 32
Discounted cash flow, 50

E

Employees, 70, 83

F

Fear, 82, 97, 101, 122
Finance, 74–78
Financial relations, 90
Ford, 15

G

Growth, 41–42, 49, 55, 85

H

High tech, 65–73, 118

I

Image, 19, 36, 87–88
Incentives, 82–83
Industrial products, 20
Inflation, 76
Investment intensity, 74–78

J

Japanese management, 92–94

L

Latecomer in market, 39,
    55–56
Learning curve, 10, 35–37, 49,
    63, 68, 77

M

Manufacturing, 65–73
Market matrix, 85
Market share, 8–10, 14–17, 23,
    31, 35, 37, 39–40, 44,
    45, 46, 49, 50, 54, 55,
    58, 63, 68, 75, 77, 83, 85
Market survey, 19
Marketing concept, 65
Marketing expenditures, 23,
    45, 77–78
Marketing mix, 20
Marketing people, 65
Mature industries, 43, 44, 45,
    50, 55, 64
Mentors, 124
Mergers, 79–81, 90
Me-tooism, 27

N

Network, 124–127
New products, 35–37, 52–56,
    57–61

P

P & L Statement, 49, 71
Packaging, 20
Pearl Harbor, 111–112
Personal experience, 114
Plant and equipment, 45,
    65–73, 76
Politics, 103, 105, 122, 124
Post hoc thinking, 115
Power, 95–118
Pricing, 30–37, 38–40
Productivity, 70–73
Profit, 8

Q

Quality, 14–25, 33, 45, 83

R

R & D, 57–61
Recessions, 70
Replacement value, 76
Robots, 43, 65, 70

S

SBU, strategic business unit, 7
Security analysts, 90
Segmentation, 62–64
Shakeout, 43, 44
Stock prices, 24, 89–91
Stockbrokers, 41–42, 44
Strategic image/personna,
    125, 128–133

T

Teams, 110–113

U

Unions, 32, 68–70

V

Value, 33–34, 38–40, 77
Vertical integration, 59–60,
    67–68
Vietnam, 112

W

Women, 119–133